Web Graphics
Visual Quick Reference

Lamont Wood

Web Graphics Visual Quick Reference

President
Roland Elgey

Senior Vice President/Publishing
Don Fowley

Publisher
Stacy Hiquet

Publishing Manager
Jim Minatel

General Manager
Joe Muldoon

Editorial Services Director
Elizabeth Keaffaber

Managing Editor
Patrick Kanouse

Acquisitions Editor
Todd Pfeffer

Product Director
Jon Steever

Senior Editor
Elizabeth A. Bruns

Editors
Kate O. Givens
Bill McManus
Sean Medlock

Strategic Marketing Manager
Barry Pruett

Webmaster
Thomas H. Bennett

Product Marketing Manager
Kristine R. Ankney

Assistant Product Marketing Manager/Design
Christy M. Miller

Assistant Product Marketing Manager/Sales
Karen Hagen

Technical Editor
Thomas McDonald

Media Development Specialist
Brandon Penticuff

Technical Support Specialist
Nadeem Muhammed

Software Relations Coordinator
Susan D. Gallagher

Editorial Assistant
Andrea Duvall

Book Designer
Kim Scott

Cover Designer
Nathan Clement

Production Team
Erin M. Danielson
Maribeth Echard
Brian Grossman
Donna Wright

Indexer
Craig Small

Composed in *Stone Serif* and *Helvetica*
by Que Corporation

About the Author

Lamont Wood has been a freelance writer in the computer and high-tech field for more than fifteen years, and has been producing corporate and special-interest Web sites since 1994. A pioneer in the use of microcomputers and telecommunications (starting, in fact, with telex machines), his first personal computer, built with a soldering iron, is now in the Smithsonian.

Dedication

To my wife, Louise O'Donnell, who understands the demands involved in writing. And to Chris and Pat, for demonstrating that twinship is powerful.

Contents

Part V   Adding Graphics to Your Web Page

Part VI   Adding Text to Web Files

Part VII Using Text and Graphics as Links

Part VIII Multiple Links per Image

Part IX Adding Backgrounds to Web Pages

Part X Animated GIFs

Part XI Multiple Columns on Pages

Part XII Using Frames with Pages

Part XIII Working with Photos

Part XIV Mounting Files on the Web

Part XV Web Graphics Tools and Sources

Files and the Web

The World Wide Web is a subset of the Internet. The *Internet*, of course, is a world-straddling network of interconnected computers and local networks that respond to a standard set of commands. Anyone sitting at an Internet computer can do certain things with any other computer on the Internet, anywhere in the world. If you have correct password access, you could practically use that computer as if you were sitting at it. But before the advent of the World Wide Web in the early 1990s, Internet access meant fetching files, usually after mastering certain arcane commands. The files would be read, viewed, processed, or run later, after the user got offline, using further software and arcane commands. Usually the only thing done online was to read short text files. While surfing was done, it demanded special expertise.

The development of the Web protocols, standards, and technologies changed all that. The following important new elements were introduced:

- Hypertext, so that one resource on the Internet could be linked to another, allowing Internet navigation without any knowledge of its commands.

- Web server software to handle the transmission over the Internet of files formatted for the Web.

- The Hypertext Markup Language (HTML) to format Web material.

- Web browser software residing on the user's machine, to format and display incoming HTML data and other information, creating a standard graphical user interface to the Web and a way to read, view, or otherwise use files while online.

- *Graphics* as part of the content, with their presentation handled by the browser software.

It is the final item—graphics—that concerns us in this book (although, as you'll see in Part VII, graphics are sometimes used as hypertext links). HTML lets you specify the use of graphics as part of the layout of a Web file or page. And indeed, the results can resemble a printed page that happens to be presented on-screen. But there are important differences that put the Web in a different league:

- Graphics can be hyperlinked—as we'll see in Part VII—to other information, either on that page, or to a file residing on the other side of the globe.

- Individual areas on a graphic can be mapped out and similarly linked to other information. For instance, you could have a graphic of a map of the country; clicking a state could bring up information about that state.

- The graphics can be animated, as we'll see in Part X.

Yes, it is possible to have a Web page without graphics. Compare these examples, which are Netscape browser screen shots of the same basic Web page file—except one includes an image.

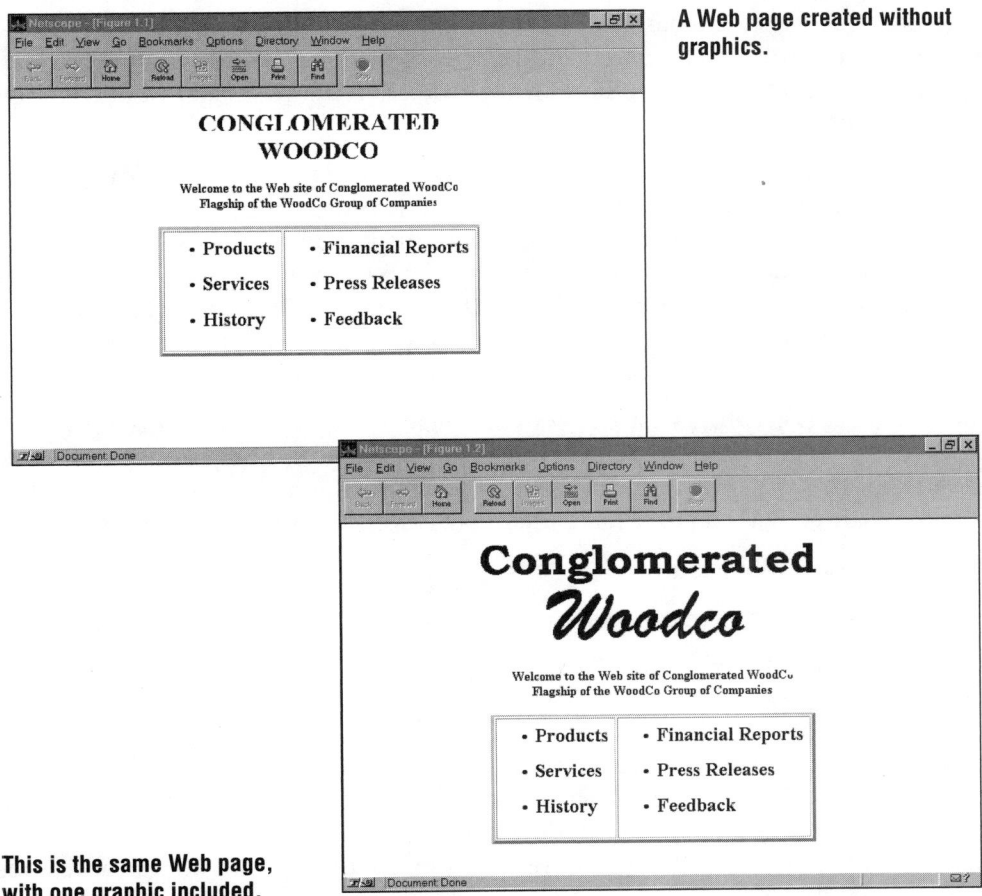

A Web page created without graphics.

This is the same Web page, with one graphic included.

As you can see, without graphics, you are limited to text. And while you can do a lot more with the text styles and fonts available on a browser than you could, say, doing the "typewriter graphics" that they used to create in the old days in high school typing classes, the results are still not as distinctive as you could get by using an image. And the image could just as easily be a corporate logo, a picture of the firm's president, a picture of the headquarters building, or anything else within reason. (You name it and someone shows an image of it on the Web.)

Also, with an image you have more control over the final appearance of the Web page. Using text, what the user sees on the screen is the result of the interaction of a number of factors, including width of the browser's window, and its default settings for font, type size, and text color. With an image, what the user sees is the image.

Control over appearance is not total, even when using an image instead of text. For example, an image can be too wide for a given screen. Or the user may not have a color monitor, may have the graphics turned off on the browser, or may not even be using a graphical browser. Things you can do about the situation will be covered as we go along (such as displaying text that will replace an undisplayed image, as discussed in Part V). If using a specific browser is advisable, many sites include a link to download the software.

In the end, it is graphics that will set your page apart, help identify the page with whatever company or organization it represents, and help establish the identity of that organization in the mind of the surfing public. And only with graphics can your Web page make use of corporate logos and symbols.

In this section, we'll examine:

- The definition of graphics files.
- Basic attributes of those files.
- How you can define those attributes.

If you have worked with graphic artists and are aware of the demands of their profession, don't be alarmed. They work with printed images that will have resolutions of more than a thousand dots per inch (dpi), and include millions of colors. On the Web, you'll be working at no more than about 100 dpi, and since browsers are limited to the display of 256 colors on 8-bit monitors, there is normally no reason to exceed that amount. If you have ordinary PC software and basic computer literacy, that will suffice.

Understanding File Types

An image used as part of a Web page is a computer file like any other. It will be transmitted from the Web server to the browser as specified by the commands contained in the HTML file that defines that page. The HTML file and the image file are two separate files. (In theory, an HTML file can use any number of image files). The browser will combine the image(s) with any data contained in the HTML file and format it and display it on the screen according to the dictates of the available resolution, fonts, colors, and so on.

The Web is possible only because of world-wide standardization. This means that files of only certain formats are used. There are four file formats that concern us:

■ *HTML files*, text files with the .htm or .html extension.

■ *GIF files*, image files with the .gif extension.

■ *PNG files*, image files with the .png extension.

■ *JPG files*, image files with the .jpg extension.

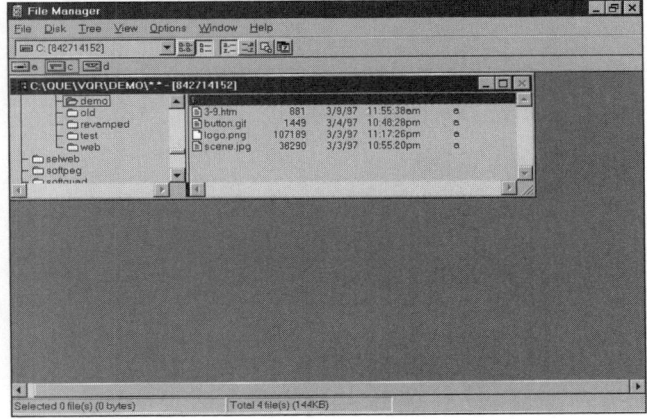

Web file types as displayed in Windows.

HTML files are text files, meaning you could read them in any word processor, or even from MS-DOS using the TYPE command. The other three are graphics files best viewed by a graphics program capable of reading that format.

It is important to understand the differences in the formats, and the uses of each. Each format is explained in detail in the following sections.

HTML Files

HTML files are not graphics files, but we must consider them because you use them to display image files. As stated, they are text files, and can be edited with essentially any text editor—the Windows Notepad will often suffice. Because they commonly reside on UNIX servers that permit longer file names, they often appear with a four-character file name extension: page.html. On Windows NT servers, the files usually have the three-character file name extension: page.htm.

A simple HTML file would look like this:

```
<HEAD><TITLE>Figure 1.4</TITLE></HEAD><BODY
<body bgcolor=white>

<CENTER>
<IMG SRC="logo.gif"><H4>Welcome to the Web site of Conglomerated WoodCo<BR>
Flagship of the WoodCo Group of Companies</H4>
<TABLE BORDER=4 CELLPADDING=8 CELL SPACING=8>
<TR><TD>
<UL>
<LI><H2>Products</H2>
<LI><H2>Services</H2>
<LI><H2>History</H2>
</TD>
<TD>
<UL>
<LI><H2>Financial Reports</H2>
<LI><H2>Press Releases</H2>
<LI><H2>Feedback</H2>
</UL>
</TD></TR>
</TABLE>
</BODY>
</HTML>
```

Look closely and you can spot the text displayed in the figure on the next page. However, it's framed by a bunch of text bracketed by the < and > symbols. Text that appears in brackets is called a *tag*; these are the formatting commands used by HTML. For instance, the tag that starts with **IMG** is used to put an image on

Note how bracketed text in the HTML file listing shows up as part of this Web page.

the page, and will be discussed in Part V. The **TABLE** tag is used to format material in columns and is discussed in Part XI.

Specific tags you'll need to know for displaying graphics will be discussed in Parts V, VI, and VII. As for the other tags, whole books have been written about the effects you can achieve with them. (Que's *Special Edition Using HTML* leaves little unsaid.) Don't be afraid to study tags and master HTML.

There are, meanwhile, graphical HTML editing packages that let you create pages without knowing HTML, and increasing numbers of desktop publishing, presentation, and word processing packages now deliver output in HTML format. While these can help you get started, they cannot satisfy every demand of every user. In the end, you'll still want to get at the raw HTML code so you can do your own fine-tuning.

Don't worry—there aren't that many tags to learn. And the results are like learning to play the piano—the number of notes on the keyboard are mercifully limited, but the music you can make is not.

GIF Files

The GIF (*Graphics Interchange Format*) format (pronounced as in jiffy) is the most common file format used on the Web, and all graphical browsers can display .GIF files. Coding the colors with 8 bits per pixel, a GIF file can include as many as 256 colors. The colors used by a GIF image are stored in a special color table inside the file, a formatting method called *color indexing*. GIF files can also be grayscale. There are two variations of GIF in use: GIF87 and GIF89a. (They are named for the year they were standardized.) Both variants allow a feature called interlacing. The later GIF89a variant allows a feature called transparency.

Transparency means that one color (usually the background color of the image) can be declared transparent. Transparency means that the background color of the Web page itself will show through, rather than the background color of the image file. That makes the image fit more naturally onto the page.

Interlacing means that the image, as it downloads over the Internet, is displayed gradually in increasing detail. The result can resemble a blurry picture that comes into focus. With interlacing, users with slower modems can usually tell what a picture is long before it completely arrives, and therefore can quickly decide whether to click it, ignore it, go back, and so on. (Users of high-speed connections, meanwhile, may never notice that you used interlacing, since the picture appears in a flash anyway. Lucky them.)

Just because fast modems have become cheap doesn't mean everyone has upgraded to one. Any time you use a GIF file, go ahead and use the interlace option.

Meanwhile, GIF87 images can still be used on the Web. They will simply lack transparency.

As we'll discuss in Part X, GIF files can also be used to create simple on-screen animations.

JPG Files

Files using the format sponsored by the *Joint Photographic Experts Group* are referred to as JPEG ("jay-peg") files, and may use a four-character filename extension on UNIX machines: image.jpeg. Formerly, not all Web browsers supported JPEG files, but this has changed. JPEG files are intended for use with photographic images. Colors are encoded with 24 bits per pixel, meaning that more than 16 million colors can be rendered. (That's easily a thousand times more colors than most people can distinguish.)

However, JPEG lacks the transparency and interlacing features available with GIF89a. (There is a feature called "progressive JPEG" that approximates the interlacing feature of GIF, but it places heavy demands on desktop computers and therefore most browsers don't support it.)

On the other hand, JPEG offers more compression than GIF, creating smaller files for the same images—when dealing with large color images or continuous tone grayscale images. For smaller, simpler images, the JPEG formats may actually create larger files than the GIF format. Also, most graphics software packages that support the JPEG format have facilities for letting you save the file by using higher levels of compression, at the expense of image quality.

PNG Files

The PNG (*Portable Network Graphics* or "ping")format is expected to achieve wide support by browsers in the foreseeable future, because it does away with the need to choose between formats. It offers the transparency and interlacing that GIF offers, but offers more colors than JPEG—up to 48 bits per pixel. Moreover, it offers moderately better compression than GIF, while not trading image quality for higher compression ratios, as JPG sometimes does.

PNG's transparency feature differs from GIF in that the degree of transparency can be variable. This allows special effects, such as images whose backgrounds fade into and merge with the background color of the page—whatever that color is. (The browser must be programmed to support this feature, of course.) PNG also includes several error-checking facilities to help ensure that an image can be edited, transmitted, and re-edited across different systems.

GIF Versus JPG Versus PNG

Basically, you should use GIF when:

- You need to use transparency in an image.

- You need interlacing.

- You have a small file (for a button or icon) and experimentation shows that the GIF version is smaller than the JPG version.

- You are using line art, or a color image with large areas of flat, unchanging color.

- You want an animation.

You should use JPG when:

- You are using a 24-bit photographic (continuous tone) images.

- You are using large, color files and experimentation has shown that the JPG version is smaller than the GIF version.

- You want to be able to choose compression levels so as to balance image quality against file size.

You should use PNG when:

- You are sure your users have browsers that can handle the PNG format.

- You want both photo-realism, and transparency or interlacing.

- You want more photo-realism than JPEG offers.

- You expect the users to capture and reuse the image.

- Size is a critical issue, and experimentation has shown that the PNG version of the file is smaller than the GIF version.

File Size Comparisons

The choice between which format to use will sometimes boil down to deciding which format produces the smallest file size. Unfortunately, there is no simple answer, since one format may work better with a particular image than another. You'll have to experiment. The following tables indicate the range of file sizes you can expect for the same image (see Tables 1.1 and 1.2).

The first image is a color image using 178 different tones, 384 pixels wide and 288 pixels high.

Color picture used for our comparisons.

Table 1.1   File Sizes with Color image

Format	File Size in Bytes
BMP (Windows bitmap)	111,760
PCX PaintBrush	148,776
GIF	48,232
JPG, standard compression	15,420
JPG, progressive compression	14,059
PNG	48,445

Notice that file sizes among the Web formats (GIF, JPG, and PNG) vary by a factor of three, and when you consider BMP and PCX (included for comparison), they vary by a factor of ten.

Next, we'll consider a black-and-white file 440 pixels wide and 145 pixels high (the logo file used earlier).

Black-and-white picture used for our comparisons.

Table 1.2   File Sizes with Black-and-White Image

Format	File Size in Bytes
BMP (Windows bitmap)	8,182
PCX PaintBrush	6,503
GIF	2,202
JPG, standard compression	16,901
JPG, progressive compression	14,704
PNG	3,742

Notice that the results vary by a factor of four. Also notice that the JPEG black-an-white image is actually the largest file by a considerable margin. In fact, it is as large as the color JPEG file. JPEG's compression algorithms are evidently counterproductive with simpler images. GIF, however, did quite well with the simpler image. PNG did about as well as GIF, as it did with the color image.

Always pay attention to the file size of your images. Beautiful pictures will not impress anyone if they have to wait five minutes for them to download.

Creating Files for the Web

We'll assume you already have an image file you want to use on the Web. Therefore, creating a Web file means converting that file into one of the Web image formats—GIF, JPG, or PNG—and adding attributes used on the Web. To do that requires the use of a graphics software program that supports these formats.

In these examples, we will use Paint Shop Pro 4.12 from JASC, Inc. Other packages can be used—and will work in a similar fashion, since to support the same file formats they must offer much the same options.

The Windows Paint utility suffices for many ordinary tasks, but it does not handle any of the standard Web graphic formats. It can read either the Windows .BMP of the PaintBrush .PCX formats, and save only in the Windows .BMP format. However, other software can be used to convert files to and from these formats.

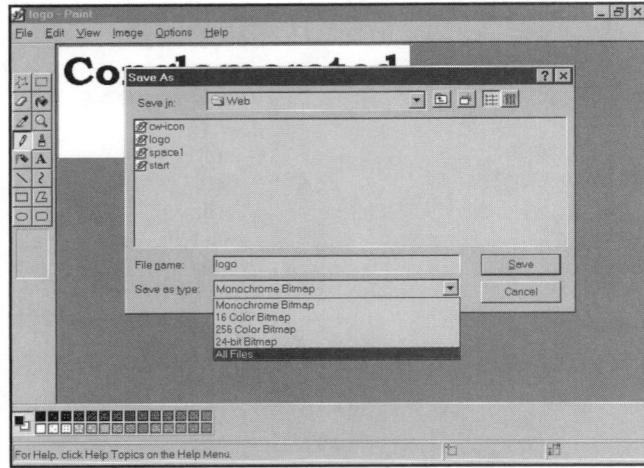

Save As options in Windows Paint: an adequate tool, but it only creates bitmap (.BMP) files.

Popular PC graphics software packages suitable for use with the Web—and how to acquire them—will be discussed in Part XV.

16

Creating GIF Files

GIF files are the mainstay of Web graphics. As mentioned in Part I, they support interlacing and transparent colors. Here, we'll bring up a logo we created using Windows Paint, in the .BMP format, and create a GIF file with it using Paint Shop Pro.

To accomplish this task, proceed as follows:

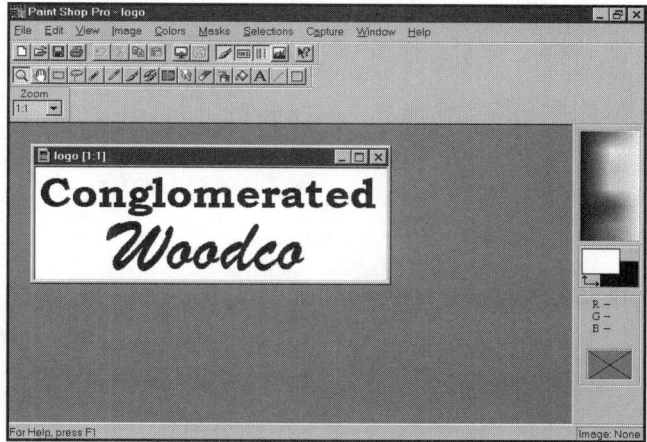

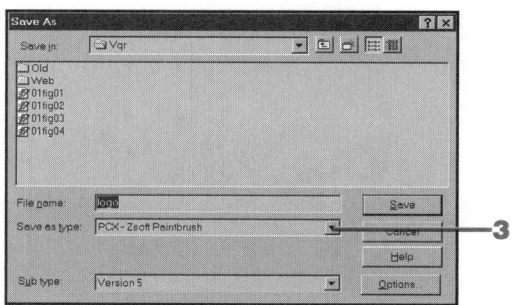

1 First, load the file in the usual way using the File and then Open command.

2 Select File, Save As. You'll get the Save As screen.

3 In the Save As screen, click the down arrow in the Save As Type, bringing up the selection box of file types.

4 Scroll through it until you see the GIF file type. (This particular program has about 30 output formats.) Click it.

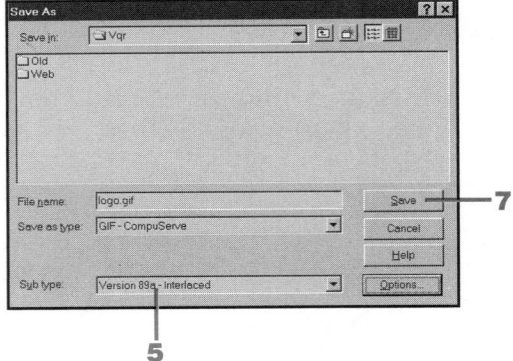

5 Likewise, in the Su̲b Type field below, click the button and select the Version 89a—Interlaced entry.

6 Be sure your screen looks something like this. Notice that in the File N̲ame field, the .GIF extension has been inserted after the file name. If you want to change the file name, do it now, but leave the .GIF extension.

7 Click the S̲ave button. You now have a GIF file that you can use for a Web page.

If you are going to create a GIF file, you might as well make it an interlaced file, as explained in Part I.

Creating Transparent GIFs

After we use the preceding GIF image we created, we may run into a problem, one best appreciated by looking at the following figure.

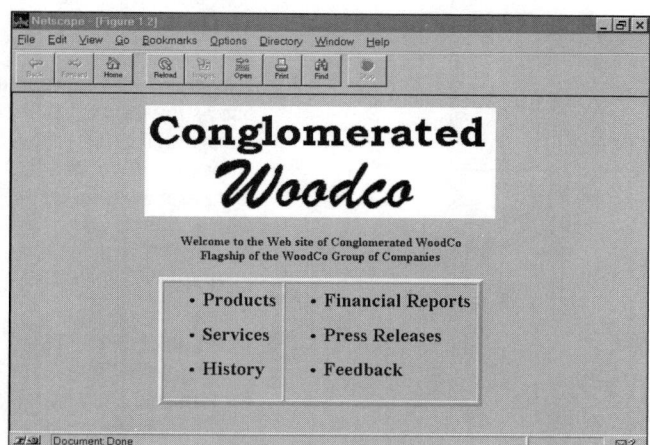

A browser screen with an image file that does not use a transparent background.

A Web page can have its own background color or image, as detailed in Part IX. (The default background color is gray, as in our example.) However, the background of the image we created is a pristine white. So the logo stands out of the page like a drive-in movie screen. But you, an aspiring graphics artist, did not consider the white rectangle that surrounds the logo to be part of the logo and wish it would go away and stop blotting out the background.

Trying to match the image's background to the page's background won't work, since there will likely be enough differences in the way the two colors are rendered to keep them from merging. Also, you may want to use a texture or image for the page's background, meaning the image's background will still stand out.

The answer is to make the background color of the image transparent. Then, the browser background will show through the image background, and the image will not stand out from the other elements in its own rectangle. To do this, use the following steps.

This is what you'll see. In our case there are only two colors, black and white, but in some images there could be far more.

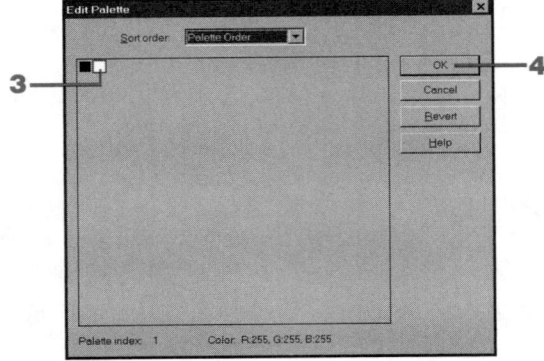

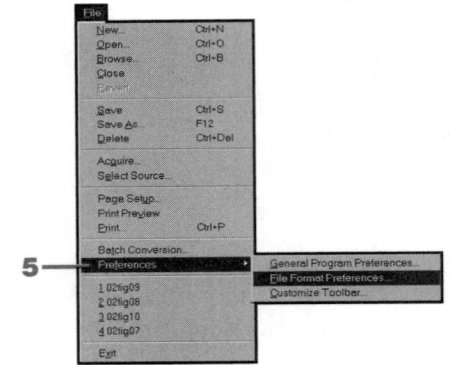

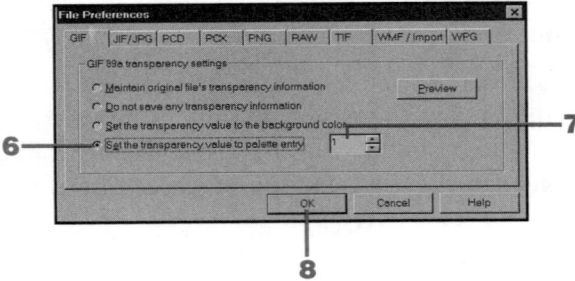

1 First, assuming you're using Paint Shop Pro, load the file in the usual way using File, Open.

2 Call up the Colors, and then the Edit Palette commands.

3 Click the color you want to use as the transparent background color. (The choice is not difficult in this case; we want white, which is entry 1.)

4 Click OK.

5 Select the File command and highlight the Preferences entry. A set of additional selections appears. Click the File Format Preferences item. The GIF settings appear by default.

6 Select the Set the Transparency Value to Palette Entry button.

7 The entry field to the right lights up. Replace the default zero to the number of the color you selected above (1, in this case.)

8 Click OK.

9 Save the file using the File and the Save As commands. As in the previous section, use the GIF file type and the Version 89a—Interlaced sub type. And the results should look like this. The logo now appears to be part of the page, rather than being inside a rectangle laid atop the page.

In Paint Shop Pro, you can target the color you want to use for the background by using the eyedropper tool to click a pixel in the image with that color. The color-in-use indicator on the right of the screen will turn that color. Click the indicator, and the color palette will come up with the color of that pixel already selected.

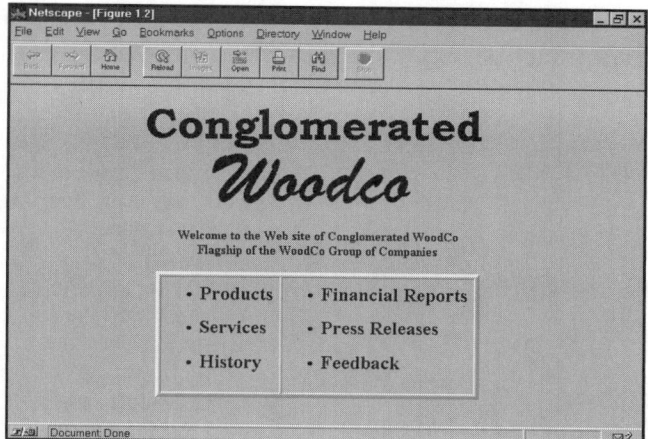

Browser screen with a GIF file that's background has been made transparent.

You can test GIF files directly using most browsers, without having to write an HTML file that uses the image. Just load the image file using the browser's File Open command. The image will appear by itself in the upper-left corner of the screen.

Creating JPEG Files

JPEG files allow fewer options—there is no transparency or interlacing—but they do offer higher compression, meaning small file sizes for the same image. If you are relying on large, complex, photo-realistic images, using JPEG can mean the difference between tolerable and intolerable download times. But as demonstrated earlier, if you are using simple two-color images, using JPG may be a mistake. Here we'll use the color image we experimented with in the file size comparison section.

1 First, load the file in the usual way using the File, Open command.

2 Select File, Save As. You'll get the Save As screen as shown here.

3 In the Save As screen, click the down arrow in the Save As Type, bringing up the selection box of file types.

4 Scroll through it until you see the JPG file type. Click it.

2

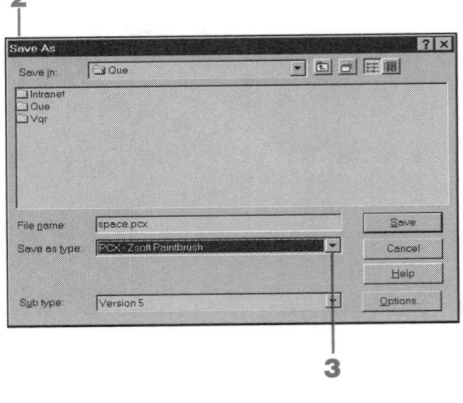

3

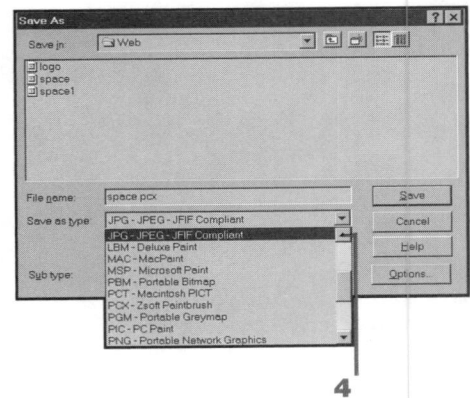

4

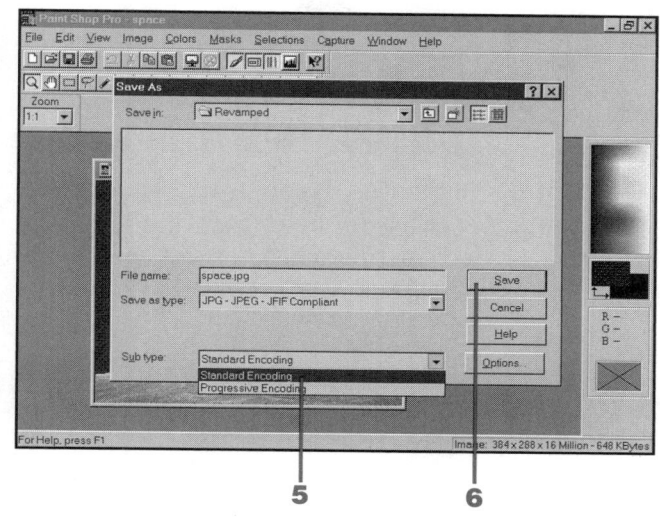

5 Likewise, in the Su̲b Type field below, click the button and select the Standard Encoding entry. (The other option, "Progressive Encoding," creates an effect rather like an interlaced GIF file, but is not yet universally supported.)

6 Click the S̲ave button. You now have a JPG file that you can use for a Web page.

Your screen should look like this. Notice that, in the File N̲ame field, the .JPG extension has been inserted after the file name. If you want to change the file name, do it now, but leave the .JPG extension.

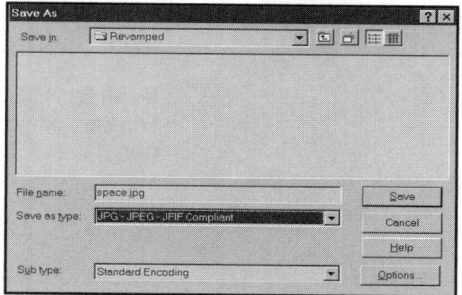

Save As screen in Paint Shop Pro, after setting options to create a JPG file.

Creating PNG Images

Creating a PNG file means saving a copy of that file in the PNG format. To do that requires the use of a graphics software program that supports the PNG format.

In this example, we will use Paint Shop Pro 4.12 from JASC, Inc., and Photoshop 4.0 from Adobe Systems, Inc. Other packages can be used—and will work in a similar fashion, because they must offer many of the same options to support the format.

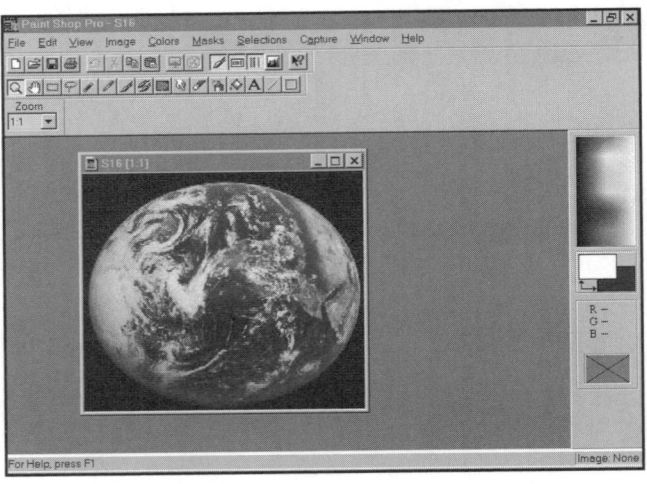

1 First, load the file by choosing the File, Open command.

2 Choose the File, Save As. You'll get the Save As dialog box shown here.

3 In the Save As dialog box, click the down arrow in the Save As Type, bringing up the list of file types.

4 Scroll through the selection box until you see the PNG file type, and then click it.

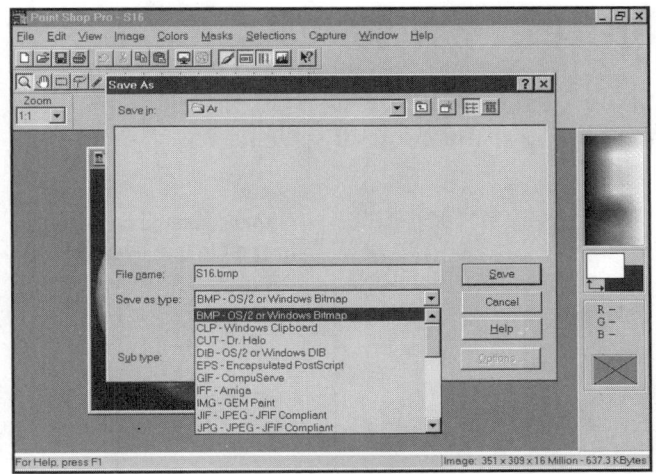

5 Likewise, in the S<u>ub</u> Type field below, click the button and select Interlaced. Your screen should look like this. Notice that in the File <u>N</u>ame field, the .PNG extension has been inserted after the file name. If you want to change the file name, do it now, but leave the .PNG extension.

6 Click the <u>S</u>ave button. You now have a PNG file that you can use for a Web page.

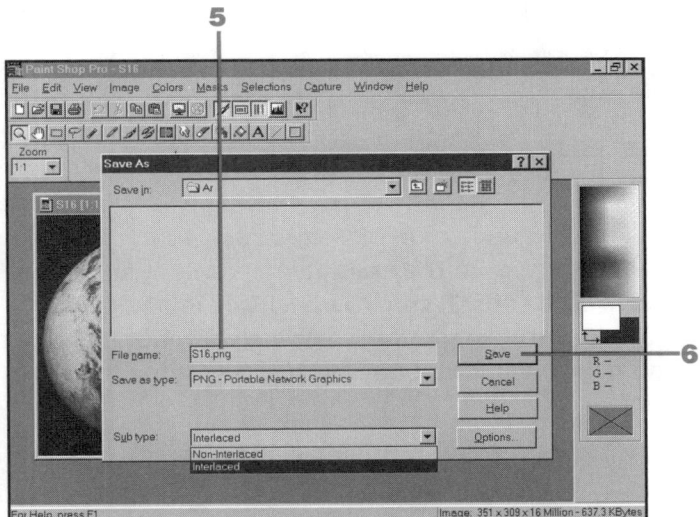

As with GIF files, if you are going to create a PNG file, you might as well make it an interlaced file. Users with slow connections will thank you.

Creating Transparent PNGs

Once we use the PNG image we created previously, we may run into a problem—one best appreciated by looking at this browser screen.

A browser screen with an image file that does not use a transparent background.

A Web page can have its own background color, or even a background image. (The default background color is gray, as in the example.) But our image has a black background, causing it to stand out. Trying to match the image's background to the page's background is unlikely to work perfectly. Even if it could, if the page uses a background image, the background of the foreground image will blot it out.

The answer is to make the background color of the image transparent. Then, the background of the page will show through the image background, and the image will not stand out from the other elements in its own rectangle.

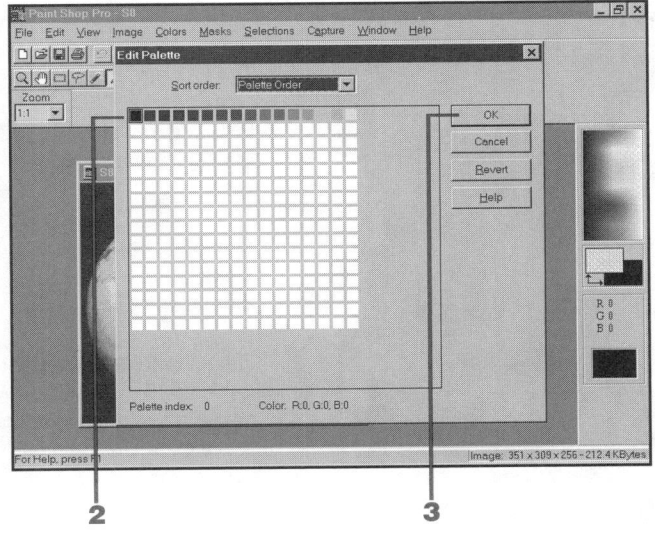

1 First, assuming you're using Paint Shop Pro, load the PNG file in the usual way using File, Open.

2 Choose Colors, Edit Palette. What you'll see is shown here. For this, 16 colors are in use.

3 Click the color you want to make transparent and then click OK.

4 Select the File and highlight the Preferences entry. A menu of additional selections appears. Choose the File Format Preferences command.

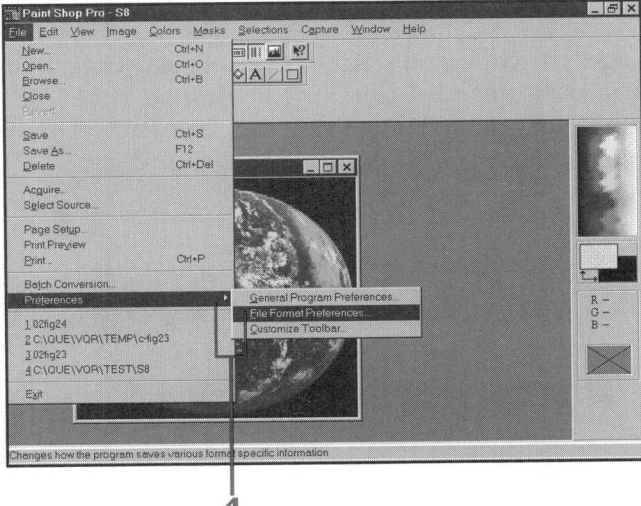

27

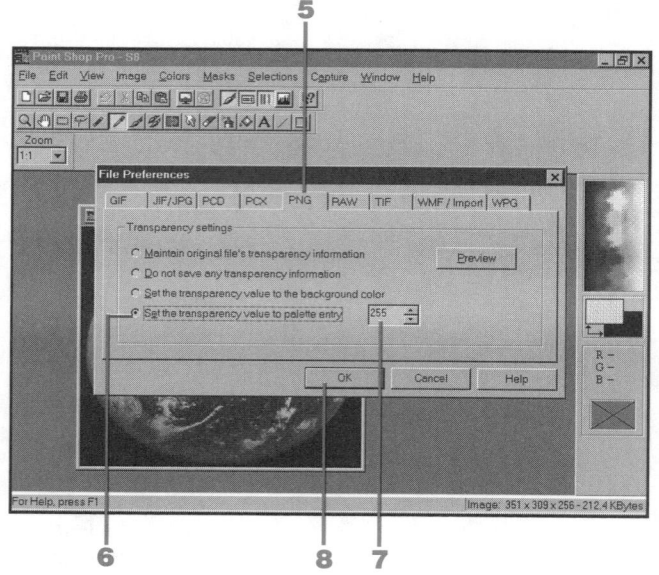

5 The File Preferences window appears. Click the PNG tab. You should see the selections shown here.

6 Select the Set the Transparency Value to Palette Entry button.

7 The entry field to the right lights up. Replace the default zero to the number of the color you selected above (255, in this case).

8 Click OK.

In Paint Shop Pro, you can target the color you want to use for the background by clicking a pixel in the image with that color using the eyedropper tool. The color-in-use indicator on the right of the screen will turn that color. Click the indicator, and the palette will come up with the color of that pixel already selected.

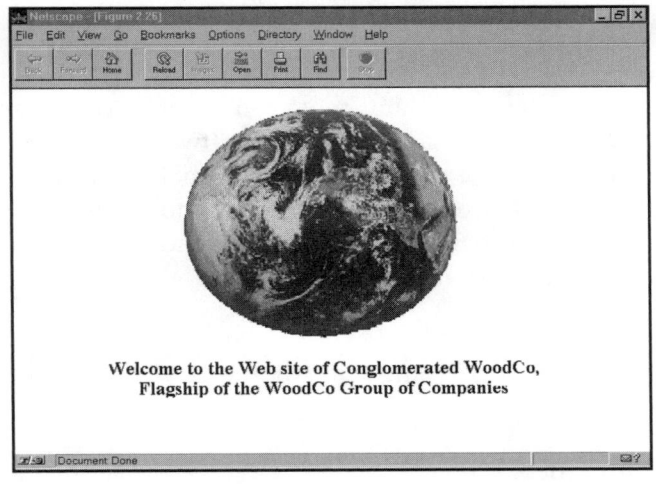

Welcome to the Web site of Conglomerated WoodCo,
Flagship of the WoodCo Group of Companies

9 Save the file using the File, Save commands. The results should look like this. The logo now appears to be part of the page, rather than being inside a rectangle laid atop the page.

29

Modifying Files

Image files, usually produced in whatever format is most comfortable to the creator, reflect the vast diversity of the graphics and authoring software available. The image files are then rendered in one of the Web formats, which are explained in Part I. Files created for other purposes (such as brochures and flyers) are often reused on the Web as well. They, too, have to be rendered in Web format, and often require other modifications, including:

- Making them smaller or larger, via resizing.
- Removal of unneeded margins, via cropping.
- Reduction of file size, often by resetting the color depth.

Part III addresses how to perform these tasks.

Format Conversions with Software

Essentially all graphics programs deal with more than one file format. The procedure for converting the format is usually simple:

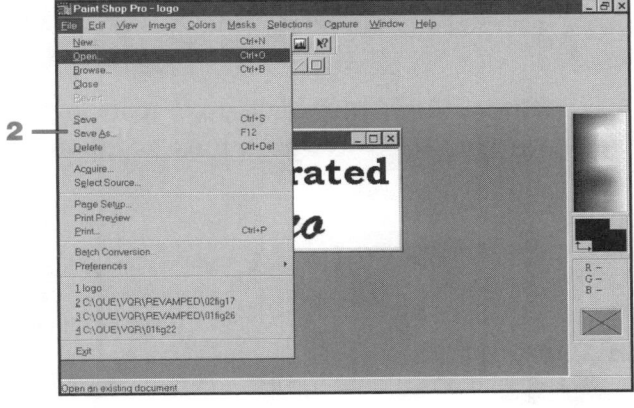

1 Load the existing file.

2 Invoke the Save As command.

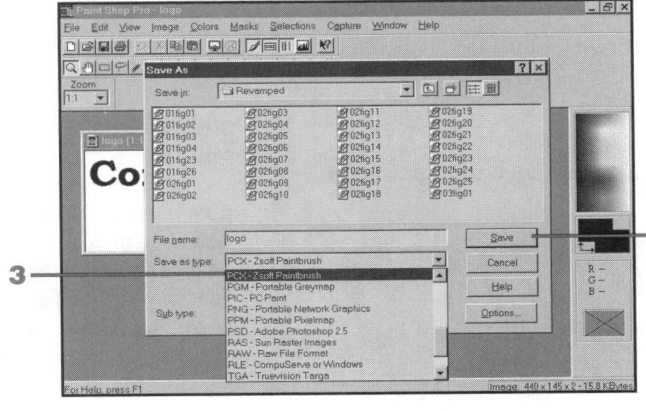

3 Select a new format from the list presented by the software.

4 Click Save.

The major consideration is: Does the software support the formats you want to use? If it does not support the format of the existing file, you can't load it. If it does not support the format to which you want to output, there is no point loading the existing file.

Before processing the conversion, the software may demand that you make certain changes, such as changing the color range or mode. With Web images, this usually is not a problem and you can simply click OK and go on.

31

Resizing Images

Suppose the boss viewed the following corporate home page and remarked that the size of the logo did not properly reflect the dignity of the firm. He wants it larger, in other words. You could start over and make a new logo. Or you could just resize it, as explained next. Most graphics packages will have some way to resize an image. For this example, we use Paint Shop Pro. Other packages will be discussed in Part XV.

Resizing means taking the image as a whole and blowing it up or reducing it, as if with a zoom lens camera. It does not mean cutting away unneeded margins. That is "cropping," which is explained later.

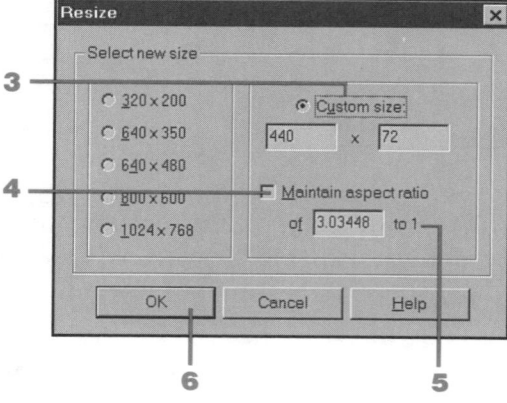

1 Load the image file you want to resize using the File and Open commands.

2 Invoke the Image and Resize commands. You'll see a Resize window.

3 Click the Custom size button.

4 Click the Maintain aspect ratio box.

5 Note the dimensions, which are in pixels. If the image is 145 pixels high and you want it a third larger, 1.33 times 145 is about 193. So you move the cursor into the box and change 145 to 193.

6 Click OK. The image changes size, as shown here. If you recall the Resize window, you'll see that the Width of the image has increased to 586, reflecting the same ratio by which the height was changed.

Maintain aspect ratio means the horizontal and vertical dimensions will be changed at an equal rate and the image will resize without any distortion. You can achieve interesting artistic effects by not maintaining the aspect ratio, but that is not what we are interested in here.

7 Now test the new file with your browser, invoking the HTML file you intend to use it with, to make sure that everything still fits on the page—and, as seen here, it barely does now.

Look carefully and you'll see that the curved lines in the enlarged logo are breaking into stairsteps. This is the inevitable result of enlarging images. Whether enlarging or shrinking a file, there is some point at which image quality becomes problematic.

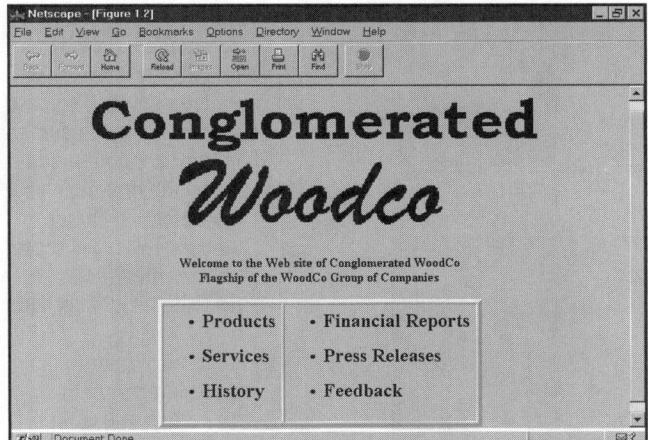

Browser screen with the new, larger image.

Part V demonstrates how to add code to the HTML file to resize an image. But results will be more consistent if you initially resize the file. Also, not all browsers support the necessary HTML functions.

Cropping Images

There usually is no reason to leave an unused margin in an image you plan to use on a Web page. The pixels that make up that blank space are bytes that have to be transmitted to the user, delaying the final arrival of the file. This is true especially when using the GIF transparency feature, where the image becomes part of the page.

Cropping is the computer-age equivalent of using scissors to remove the excess paper around the image you want to use. We'll assume you are using Paint Shop Pro.

1 You've taken a liking to a certain government high-altitude photo of your home. You load it using the File, Open commands, as shown here.

2 Click the Selection tool icon in the toolbar. (It's the one with the dotted rectangle in it. If you are unsure, leave the cursor on it for a moment and see what label pops up.) The Selection cursor appears—a heavy cross with a dotted rectangle in the bottom-right corner.

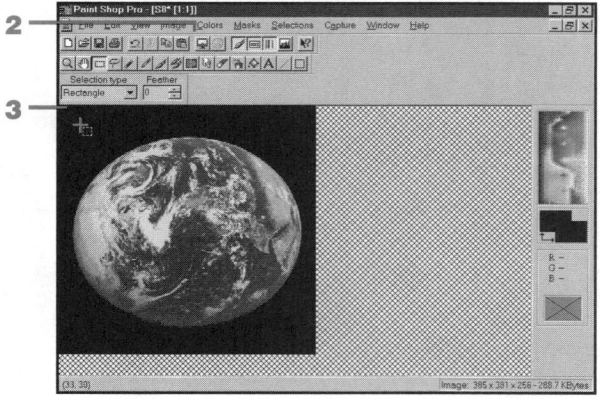

3 Place the cursor in the upper-left corner of the rectangular area of the image that you want to keep.

But there is a black expanse at the top and bottom of the image. It just takes up space and wastes bytes. So you decide to crop the image into a square around the big ball in the center.

4 Click-drag the icon to the lower right of the area you want to save. The area will now be surrounded by a thin line, as shown here.

5 Release the mouse button. The area to be saved is now surrounded by a heavier, dotted line.

6 Select Image, Crop. The image outside the "crop mark" disappears, as shown here.

7 You can now save the image under its old name or a new one, with its old format or a new one.

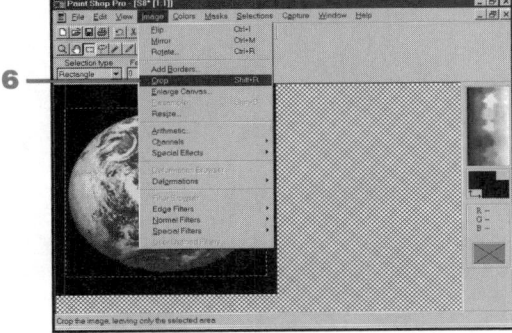

6 —

Tips for Reducing File Size

If a page takes a tediously long time to load, you can bet that image files are causing the bulk of the delay. However, the following steps can be taken to reduce the size of individual files:

1. Experiment with the three different Web formats, as described, concerning the size file they produce from the same image.

2. Crop unused margins, as described in Part III.

3. Resize, to make them smaller, as described in Part III.

4. Change color depth, as described in the two following sections.

You cannot reduce the color depth in a JPG file because the JPG format only 24-bit depth for color images—but its compression ratios may make it competitive with GIF or PNG on a given image. For grayscale images, it uses 8 bits.

Setting GIF Color Depth

GIF images can be saved as either 8-bit (256 colors or grayscale); four-bit (16 colors), or one-bit (stark black-and-white) images. There are images where the difference between 256 and 16 colors is not evident, and using 16-bit color depth in such situations will reduce the file size. Two-bit depth is useful mostly for diagrams and line drawings.

After reducing color depth, some specific colors may no longer be in use. If you were using a transparent color (as described in Part II), check to see if the transparency information is still valid.

To change the color depth of a GIF file, proceed as follows:

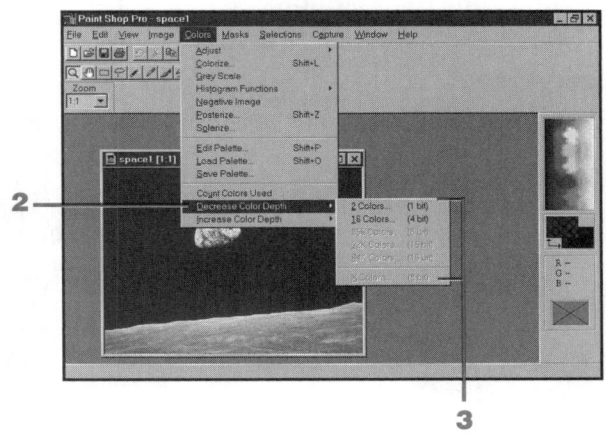

1 Load the image by using the File, Open command.

2 Select Colors, Decrease Color Depth commands as shown.

3 Select one of the available color depths. (Because this image started at 256 colors, it can be converted to only 16 or 2 colors.)

4 Save the file.

Saving the image used in the previous cropping example results in the following file sizes shown in Table 3.1.

Table 3.1   GIF File Sizes at Different Color Depths

Color Depth	File Size in Bytes
8-bit (256 colors)	87K
4-bit (16 colors)	37K
grayscale	37K
1-bit (black/white)	5K

37

Setting PNG Color Depth

Setting PNG color depth is similar to setting GIF color depth (as detailed in the previous section) except that PNG handles 16-bit color as well. PNG images can be saved as either 16-bit (64,000 colors), 8-bit (256 colors or grayscale); four-bit (16 colors), or one-bit (stark black-and-white) images. Some images show no difference between the 16-bit, 8-bit, and 4-bit versions. Choosing the 4-bit version deflates the file size with no evident loss of image quality. (Of course, 2-bit depth is useful mostly for diagrams and line drawings.)

After reducing color depth, some specific colors may no longer be in use. If you were using a transparent color (as described in Part II), check to see if the transparency information is still valid.

To change the color depth of a PNG file, proceed as follows:

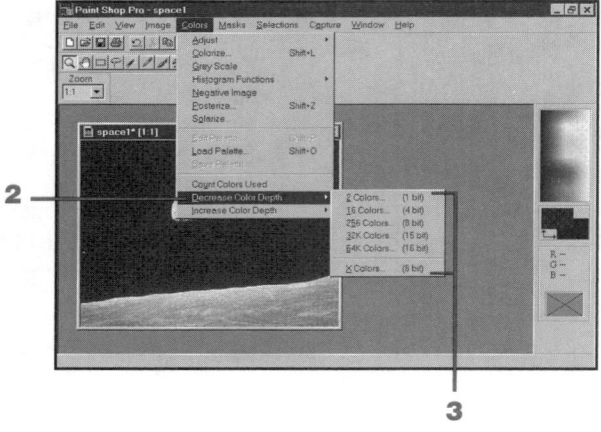

1 Load the image by using the File and Open commands.

2 Invoke the Colors and then the Decrease Color Depth commands as shown.

3 Select one of the available color depths. Because this image started at 64,000 colors, it can be converted to 32,000 colors (rarely used), 256 colors, 16 colors, or two colors.

4 Save the file.

Saving the image used in the previous cropping example results in the following file sizes shown in Table 3.2.

Table 3.2   PNG File Sizes at Different Color Depths

Color Depth	File Size in Bytes
16-bit (64,000 colors)	107K
8-bit (256 colors)	41K
4-bit (16 colors)	39K
grayscale	39K
1-bit (black/white)	6K

Creating Icons and Buttons

Consider this Web page:

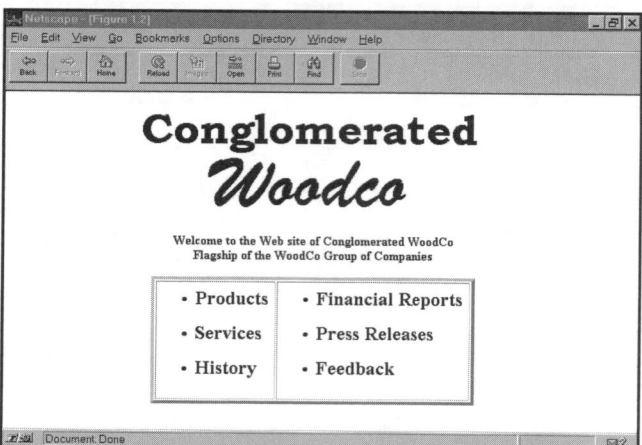

Bland Web page lacking any icons or buttons, or other evidence of creativity.

It gets the job done, but it's rather, well, bland. In terms of Web artistry, it hardly keeps up with the Joneses. And what the Joneses are doing is using icons and buttons for their links, instead of the bullets used here. And please don't roll your eyes and make remarks about "everyone wants to be Picasso" and "some pages look like ransom notes." Both are true—but nevertheless there are perfectly good reasons for using icons and buttons:

- They're more attractive, adding color and imagery to the page.

- They can help create a unified image, using the same color scheme and graphical motif.

- They can be used to help navigation, with different schemes for different links (the highlighted material that causes you to jump when clicked).

- Having a block of text that's entirely underscored (as a hyperlink) looks clumsy—especially as you can just link to the associated icon.

- Icons and buttons, as we'll show, are not that hard to make.

An **icon** is a small logo. It is intended to cause adjacent material to stand out. It may or may not do anything when you click it. A **button** is a more elaborate icon, often made to actually look like a push-button, perhaps with 3-D effects.

The icon/button is the small image you click with the mouse cursor to invoke a link. You can have links without icons, but using an icon calls it out more effectively than just having some text that happens to be underlined and colored.

Icons are usually about 35 pixels square, but there is no hard and fast rule. As you gain experience, you may find yourself making them bigger or smaller. If you want to put your boss's face in the icon, you may want to make it bigger. If you want it to fit inside a line of body text, you may make it smaller.

We'll assume you are using Paint Shop Pro, although other packages (discussed in Part XV) will do perfectly well.

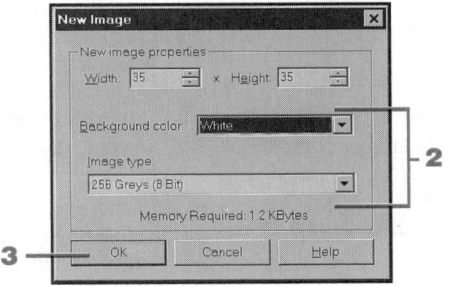

1 Begin a new file using the File and then the <u>N</u>ew commands.

2 In the New Image dialog windows, set the width and height to 35 pixels, and the background to white. (And since this is a black-and-white book, we made this a grayscale image.) If there is a color depth you want (discussed in Part III), you can use this window to set it.

3 Click OK. You'll see a tiny work area on the screen.

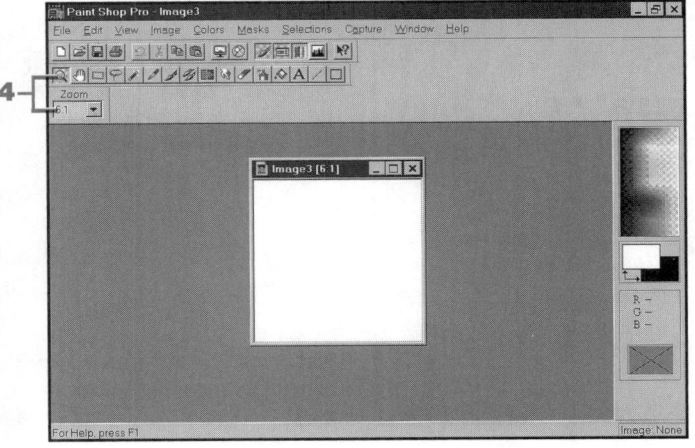

4 Use the zoom command to blow it up with either the zoom tool or the zoom selection box. About 6:1 (six to one) should be comfortable, as shown here.

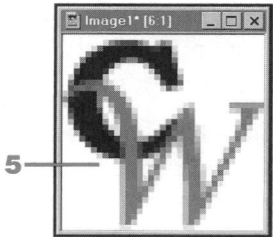

Use colors that are consistent with the rest of your artwork, but plan on making the background transparent, so that that backgrounds of the icons will merge into the background of the page.

Presentable icons can be generated quickly using text. The Windows symbol fonts are also rich sources of instant icons. For notes on using photos and colors, see Part XIII.

The Web page can now look like this—and has a little more pizzazz.

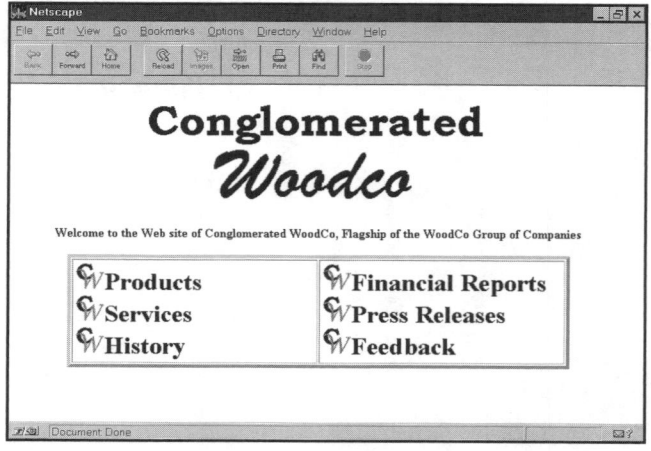

5 You can now perform any graphical function that you could perform on a full page—the results will just be smaller. This includes drawing something from scratch, or incorporating an existing image—presumably one that's been reduced in size. If you do not feel competent for the former, or have no suitable image for the latter, you can create an icon from the character sets of various fonts, as detailed in the subsequent "Working with Text in an Image," section.

6 When you are finished, zoom down (clicking the right mouse button with the zoom tool selected) to the 1:1 ratio to see if you like the results.

7 Assuming you're satisfied, save it as a GIF file with a transparent background, as described in Part II.

Web page with icons added, demonstrating reduced blandness.

The HTML coding necessary to add icons and buttons to a page will be demonstrated in Part V.

Creating Basic Buttons

Buttons are basically fancier icons. They are used for the same purpose, but you go to the effort to make them look more like buttons, enhancing the impact of your page and justifying your salary.

And now we're getting into the realm of genuine artistry, and there are an infinite number of directions to proceed. The problem, in fact, may be deciding when to stop fiddling with the thing and post the file. Ultimately, we can't help you there, but we can point you in several directions by which you can create a button with minimal hassle.

With Paint Shop Pro there's a "buttonizing" function to make it look like a three-dimensional button.

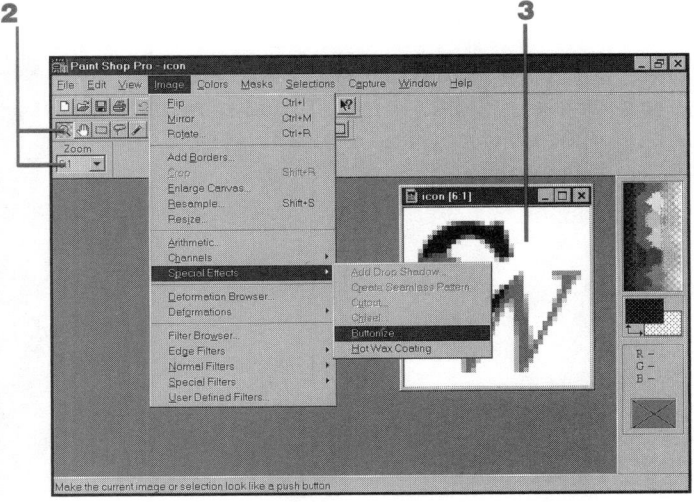

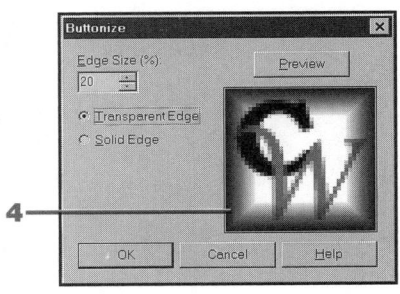

1 Load the icon you want to turn into a button using the File and Open commands.

2 Enlarge the image until it is comfortable to work with. You can either invoke the zoom tool and then click the image to make it bigger, or use the zoom selection box.

3 Select the Image and then the Special Effects commands. You'll see a list of options. Click the Buttonize option.

4 You'll see the Buttonize window, as shown here. You can accept the image as is, or experiment with the other options.

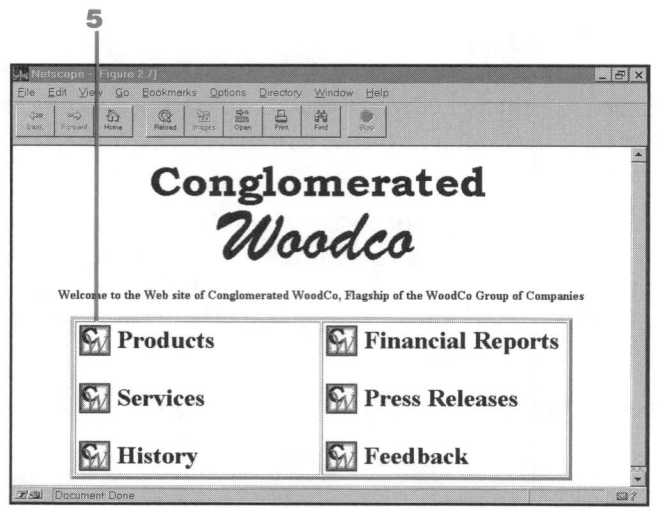

5 Zoom down to 1:1 to examine the results.

6 If you want a transparent background, set the transparency values as explained in Part II. Any transparency value in the original image will be inherited by the edited one.

7 Save it using the File and the Save commands.

Our icon is actually not that well-suited for buttonizing—you might want to use smaller, centered elements that do not bleed over into the shadowed margins, as our logo does. However, that's more of a consideration with larger buttons.

Creating Drop-Shadow Buttons

The Drop-shadow effect means that a shadow is "dropping" from the image, making it look like it is an object suspended just above the page. Paint Shop Pro has a special effects filter that does this automatically. You can do it with an icon or button, and here we'll use the button we just created:

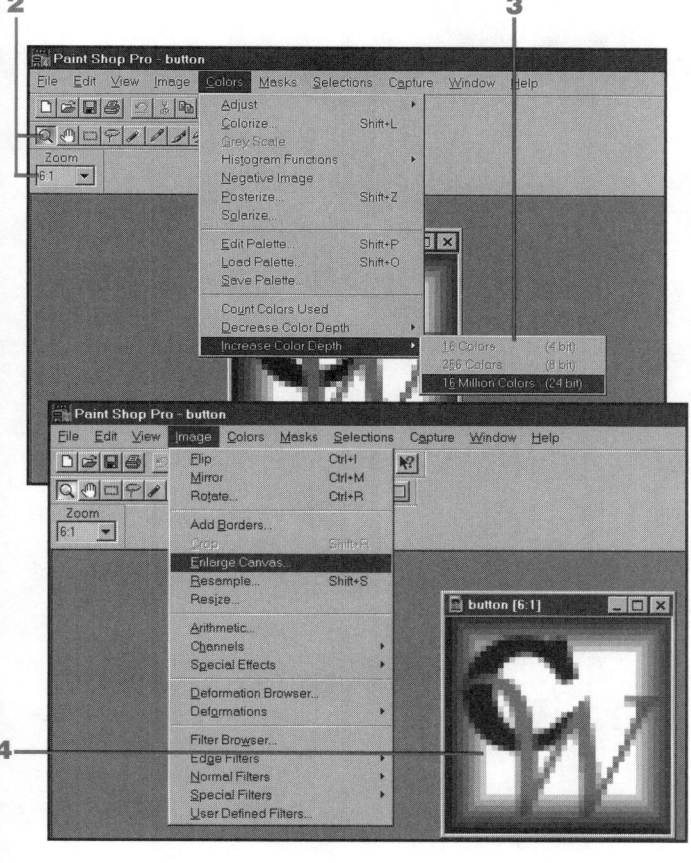

1 Load the icon you want to turn into a drop-shadow button using the File and Open commands.

2 Enlarge the image until it is comfortable to work with. You can either invoke the zoom tool and then click the image to make it bigger, or use the zoom selection box.

3 Select the Colors and then the Increase Color Depth commands, and select 16 Million Colors.

4 The shadow takes up room, so we have to enlarge the image. Select the Image and then the Enlarge Canvas commands.

5 You'll see the Enlarge Canvas dialog box, as shown here. Add about ten to both the Width and Height values.

6 Click OK. You'll see the new image in a larger window, as shown.

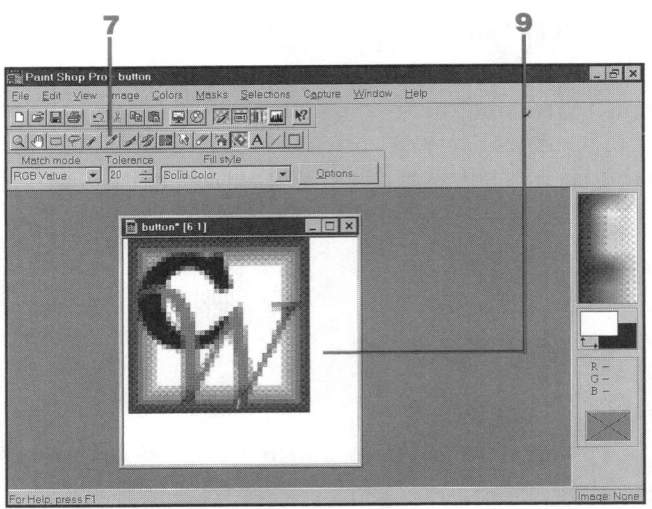

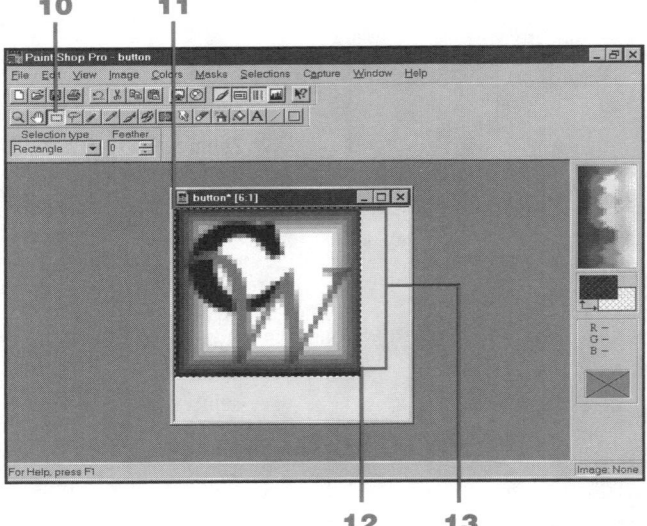

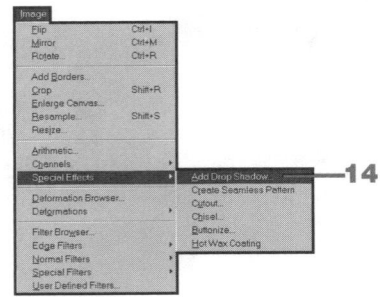

7 If you like the color of the new background, skip to Step 10. Otherwise, change it using the eye-dropper. Click the eye-dropper tool. Place the resulting eye-dropper cursor on some point in the image that uses the background color you want. Click.

8 Click the Flood Fill tool.

9 Move the new cursor to the newly added image area that has the wrong color, and click.

10 Select the area to be shadowed. First, click the selection tool.

11 Place the selection cursor in the top-left corner of the original button or icon.

12 Drag the cursor to the bottom right of the original image, so that it is surrounded by the selection mark.

13 Let go of the button. The image should now be surrounded by a pulsing dashed line, as shown here.

14 Select the Image and then the Special Effects commands. A list of special effects appears. Select the Add Drop Shadow item.

The Drop Shadow command window appears, as shown here.

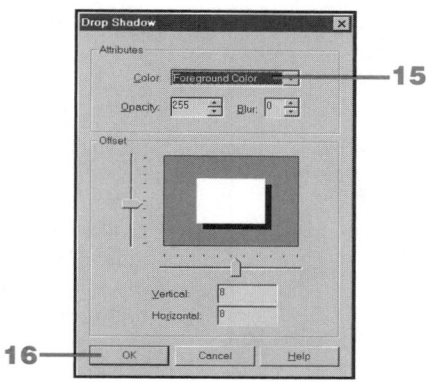

15

16

15 Change the attribute color (for the shadow itself) to black. We'll assume the other attributes are acceptable.

16 Click OK. The results should resemble this, with a shadow added on the lower right and the rest of the new areas of the image in the background color.

Don't be afraid to play with the other Drop Shadow settings. The Opacity attribute determines how dark the shadow will be, and the Blur attribute controls how sharp the edges of the shadow will be. But if more than one icon/button on the page is to have drop shadows, try to give them all the same attributes.

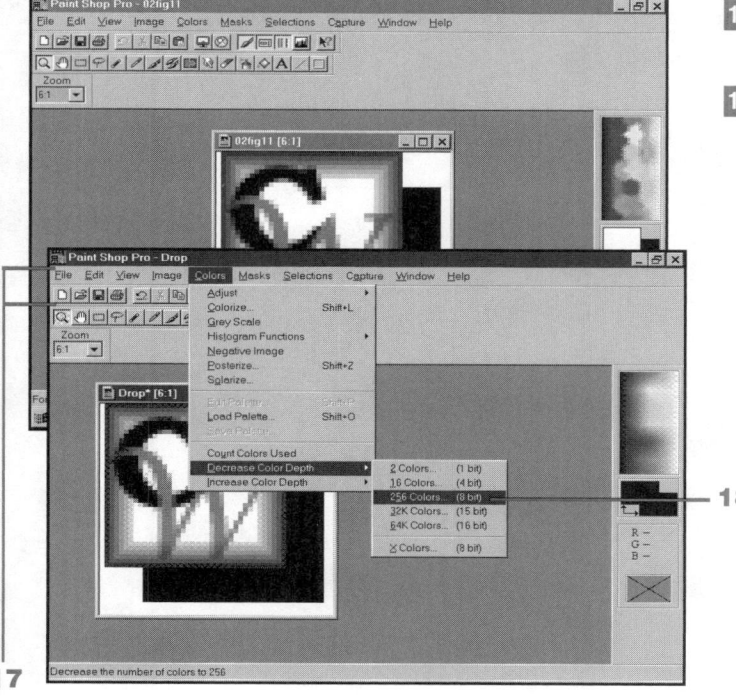

17 Zoom down to 1:1 to examine the results.

18 Reset the color depth to what it was originally— probably 256 colors. Select the Colors and then the Decrease Color Depth commands, and then select 256 Colors.

18

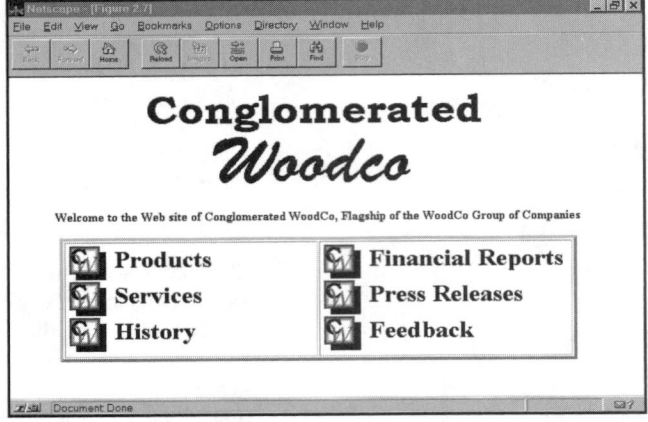

19 The Decrease Color Depth window appears. The default values normally suffice. Click OK.

20 Save your new drop-shadow button as a GIF file using the File and the Save commands, as explained in Part II. If you want a transparent background, and it was not already transparent in the original image, set the transparency values as explained in Part II.

21 If you are saving it under a different name, you will have to change your HTML coding to use the new file, as was done here.

If more than one icon/button on the page is to have drop shadows, try to give them all the same attributes.

Creating Embossed Images

Embossing is the kind of raised lettering used on engraved invitations—and you can give your page a similar impact without having to pay a printer. All you have to do is add the embossing effect, which is available via Paint Shop Pro.

Embossing is probably more effective for larger images and icons than buttons, so we'll try it with an icon.

The embossing effect depends on the contrast between the black-and-white edges of the image and a grayish background. It will not work if you are using a white or black background. For background colors other than gray, you will want to experiment.

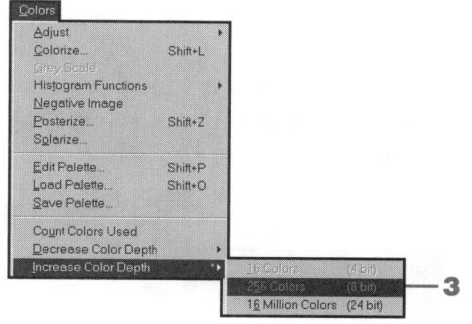

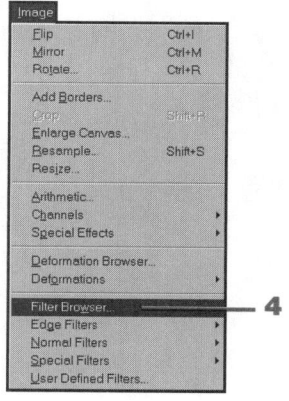

1. Load the icon you want to emboss using the File and Open commands.

2. Enlarge the image until it is comfortable to work with. You can either invoke the zoom tool and then click the image to make it bigger, or use the zoom selection box.

3. For Paint Shop Pro to do what we are going to do, the image has to have a color depth of at least 256 colors. It probably already does. If not, select the Colors and then the Increase Color Depth commands, and select 256 Colors.

4. Select the Image and then the Filter Browser commands. You'll see the Filter Browser window.

49

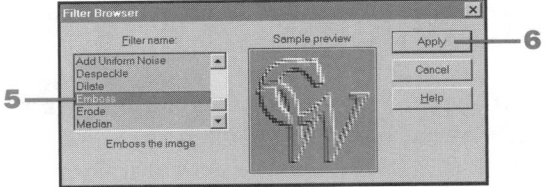

5 Scroll down the list of fil-ters until you see the Emboss entry, and click it. The window's preview screen will now show what the image will look like—a gray back-ground with an image that appears to rise from it, as shown here.

6 Click Apply. The Filter Browser screen goes away and the image looks like the preview did.

The background color used by the embossing effect is probably not the same color used by the original image. If not, follow the next seven steps:

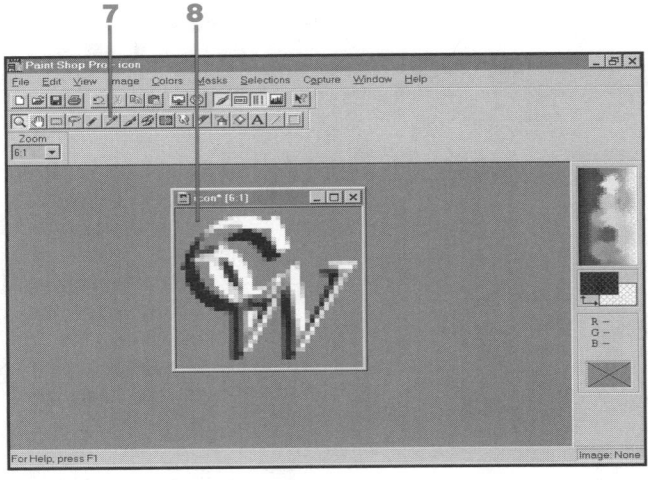

7 Select the eyedropper tool.

8 Place the eyedropper cur-sor at some point in the image that contains the gray background color used by the embossing effect. Click the right mouse button, not the left one that you usually use. This will set Paint Shop Pro's Background Color to the color of the pixel you clicked.

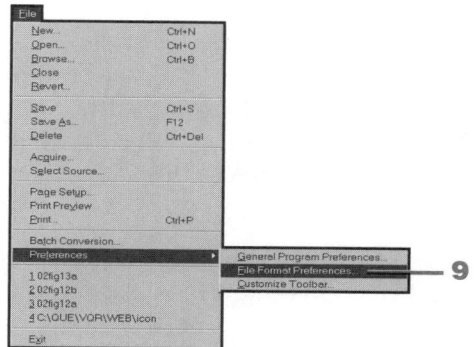

9 Select the File, Preferences, and File Format Preferences commands.

10 The File Preferences window appears. Make sure the GIF tab is selected.

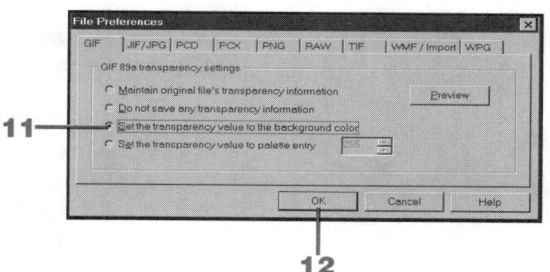

11 Click the radio button of the Set the Transparency Value to the Background Color item. (This sets the transparency value to the color selected earlier using the eyedropper.)

12 Click OK.

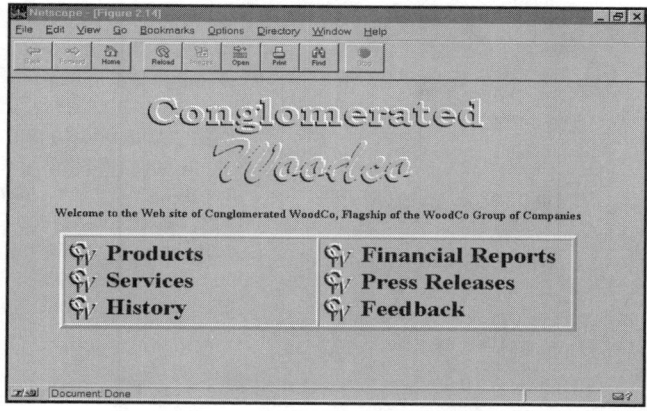

13 Save the file in the GIF format as described in Part II. The results can look like the figure to the left.

Web page employing an embossed logo and icons. Note the use of the gray background.

Background colors for Web pages, and how to add them, will be covered in Part IX.

Using Gradients and Fill

Fill means to paint in a color, usually in the background, although you can fill solid, contiguous image elements also. A gradient is a fill color that is not solid, but spans a spectrum, like a rainbow. You can have a linear gradient, or sunburst or rectangular patterns. We'll try one in Paint Shop Pro.

Fill and gradients are more suited to things like dividers—a long narrow line a few pixels deep, separating vertical elements—and to background patterns. Background patterns will be covered in Part IX.

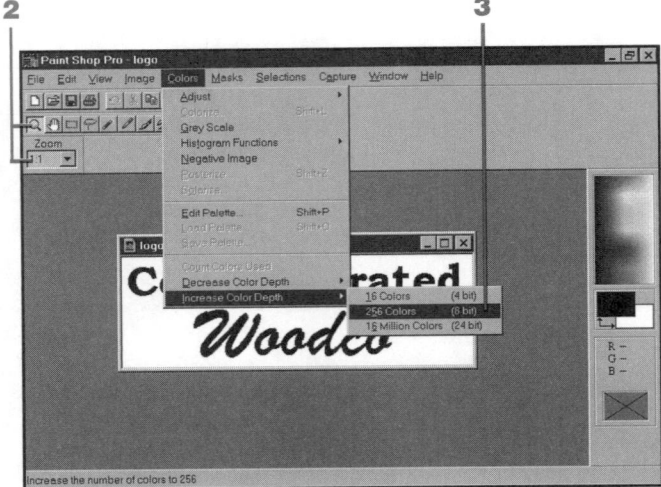

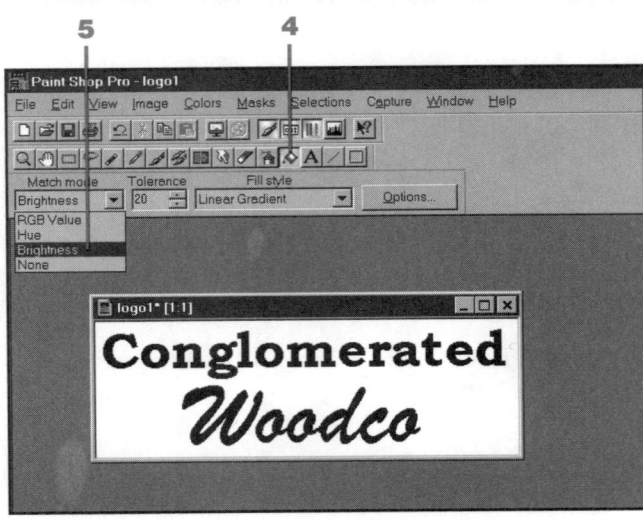

1 Load the icon or other image that you want to manipulate using the File and Open commands.

2 Enlarge the image until it is comfortable to work with. You can either invoke the zoom tool and then click the image to make it bigger, or use the zoom selection box.

3 For Paint Shop Pro to do what we are going to do, the image has to have a color depth of at least 256 for grayscale and 16 million for color images. If it does not, select the Colors and then the Increase Color Depth commands, and select either 256 Colors or 16 Million Colors.

4 Select the Flood Fill tool (the pouring paint can). Several options appear below the tool.

5 Select "Brightness" for Match Mode.

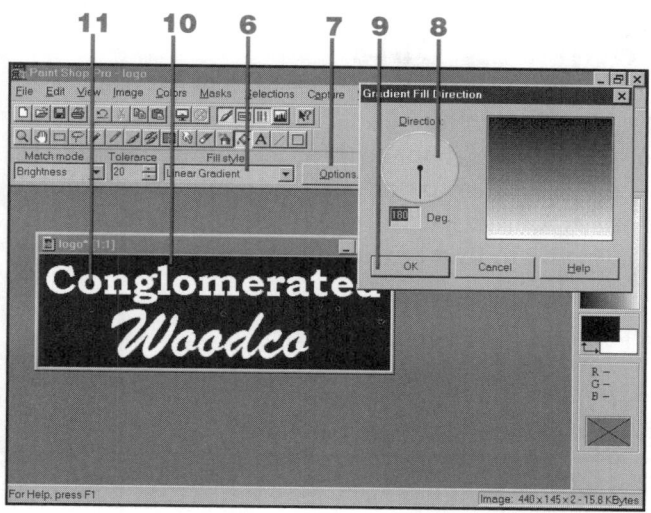

The image has been converted to negative image to show the effects better. Use the Colors and then the Negative Image commands if you want to do this.

Take time to experiment. Using colors, effects can be created that we can only hint at here in black and white.

6 Select "Linear Gradient" for Fill Style.

7 Several attribute selections appear below it. Click the Options button.

8 You'll see a direction clock indicating which way the pattern will run. You can set the numeric data or move the clock hand. (As shown, we used 180 degrees, with the color fading toward the bottom.)

9 Click OK.

10 Put the Flood Fill cursor in whatever part of the image you want filled with gradient (presumably, the background) and click.

11 If there are *voids* in the image not touched by the flood-fill (such as the inside of the letters in this case), carefully click inside them, too. The fill inside will match the fill outside.

12 Save the image using the File and Save commands. Transparent colors will probably not be an issue.

Using Other Special Effects

Most graphic packages these days will offer additional "distortion" filters that may prove interesting if used on an icon. (To make things additionally interesting, the effect of a distortion can be limited to one part of an image using the Selection tool.) Some distortions amount to additional three-dimensional effects. Others may prove challenging to find any use for, frankly. But you're the artist—use your imagination.

Distortion filters available in Paint Shop Pro are included in Table 4.1.

Table 4.1 Paint Shop Pro Deformation Filters

Filter	Effect
Circle	Images appears to be pasted atop a ball.
Cylinder-Horizontal	Image appears to be on a sideways cylinder.
Cylinder-Vertical	Image appears to be on an upright cylinder.
Motion Blur	Horizontal blurs are added to the image.
Pentagon	Image appears to be pasted atop a pentagon.
Perspective-Horizontal	Image becomes smaller toward the left.
Perspective-Vertical	Image becomes smaller toward the top.
Pinch	Image appears compressed toward the center.
Punch	Image appears to push out at the center.
Skew	Image appears tilted to the upper right.
Wind	Horizontal blur, but less than the Motion Blur.

Now, let's actually put this to work. We'll use the button we created in the "Using Text in an Image" section and create something unique.

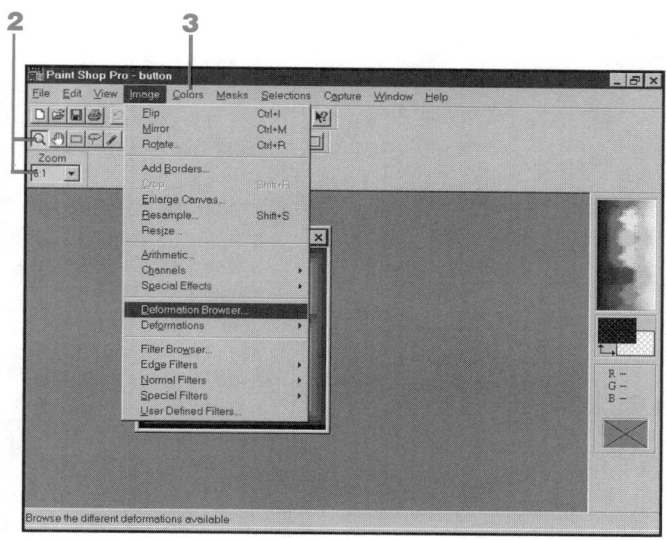

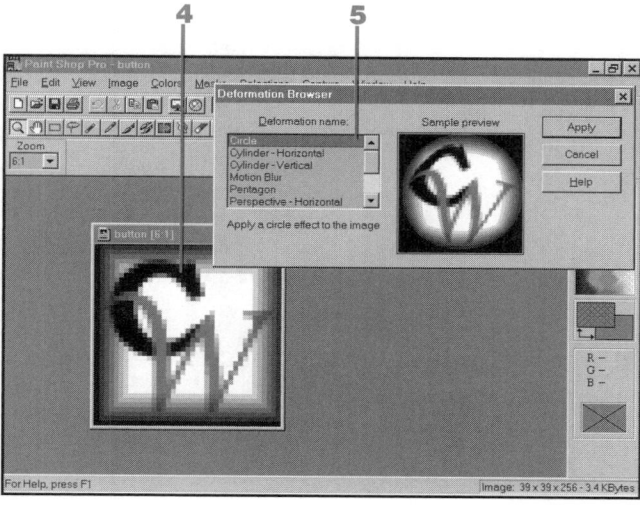

1 Call up the file using the File and the Open commands.

2 Enlarge the image until it is comfortable to work with. You can either invoke the zoom tool and then click the image to make it bigger, or use the zoom selection box.

3 Use the Colors and Increase Color Depth commands to raise the color depth to 16 million. (You'll undo this later.)

4 Select the Image and then the Deformation Browser commands. The Deformation Browser control window appears, as shown.

5 Scroll through the list of deformations. The preview screen shows the effect of each one on your image.

6 Decide which one you like. (We chose the Circle deformation.)

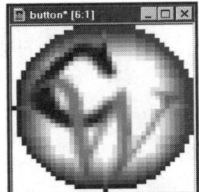

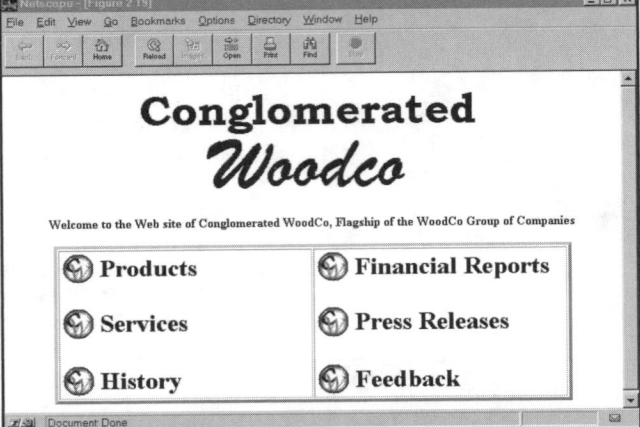

7 Click Apply. The original image now looks like the preview window looked—and you have a logo that looks like it is on a ball.

8 The image margins outside the ball need to be transparent. Use the eyedropper tool to click a point in the image that uses the transparent color, and then use the flood-fill tool to recolor the margin areas. The results are shown here.

9 Zoom down to 1:1 to see if you like the results.

10 Use the Colors and Decrease Color Depth commands to change the color depth back to what you were originally using: probably 256 colors.

11 Save the file as a GIF image, as described in Part II.

Don't be afraid to combine filters and deformations. But remember—at some point, you have to declare the project finished and quit.

Working with Text in an Image

While it helps if you do, you don't need any particular skill as an artist or illustrator to create perfectly good icons. That's because you don't need to draw anything, since a wealth of preexisting graphical symbols is built into Windows in the character sets of the various fonts.

In this section, we'll use those fonts to quickly generate an icon. In this case, we have noticed that the Conglomerated Woodco logo uses text in two distinct fonts. So it's natural to have an icon with the initials CW and those fonts.

To create such an icon out of text, proceed as follows:

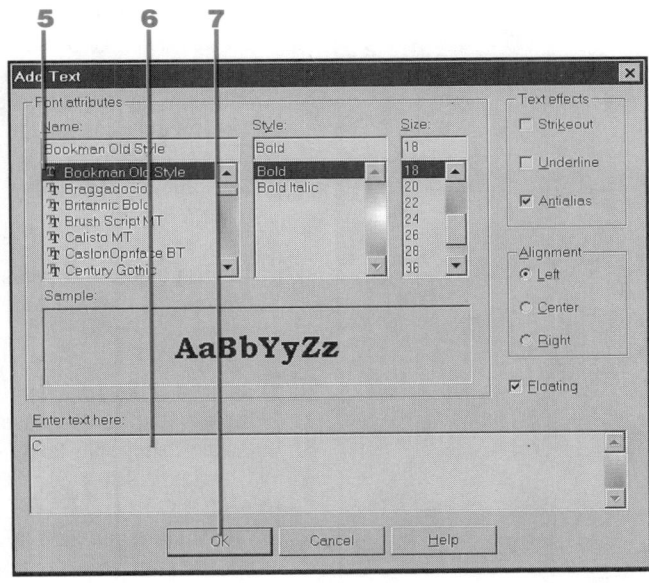

1 Open a new graphics file, size it, and zoom in, as detailed in the earlier "Creating an Icon" section.

2 Select a color you want to use for the first letter, click the "eye dropper" tool and then click the color chart. In this case we chose black.

3 Click the Text tool.

4 The text tool icon appears. Click inside the work area with it. You'll see the Add Text dialog windows, as shown here.

5 Select a heavy serif type for the C. As shown, we chose Bookman Old Style bold, 18-point.

6 Type the text you want in the text entry area—in this case, the single letter C.

7 Click OK.

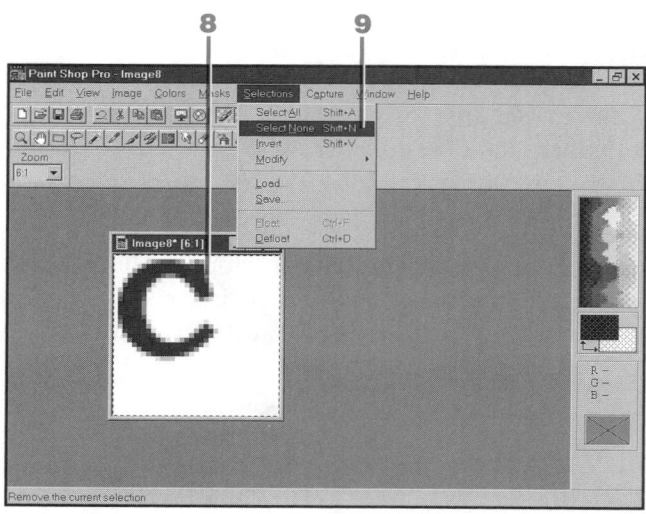

8 You'll be returned to the work area with the letter in outline form within, as shown. Move the cursor to position the letter in the upper-left corner of the work area.

9 Deselect the letter by invoking the Selections and then the Select None commands.

10 Select a color for the second letter: Again, invoke the dropper tool and click another color. We chose some lighter color, which will show up as gray since this is a grayscale image.

11 Click the Text tool. (The letter A in a box.)

12 The text tool icon appears. Click inside the work area with it.

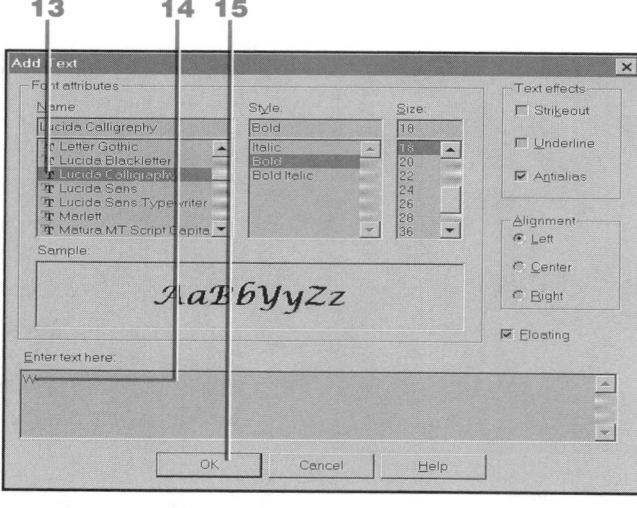

13 Select a calligraphic font for the letter W. We chose Lucida Calligraphy bold, 18-point.

14 Type the text you want in the text entry area—in this case, the single letter W.

15 Click OK. You'll be returned to the work area with the letter in outline form within it. Move the cursor to position the letter in the lower right of the work area. It will appear to be atop the C.

Deselect the letter by invoking the **S**elections and then the Select **N**one commands.

The result may resemble this. Zoom down to the 1:1 ratio to see if you like the results.

Assuming you're satisfied, save it as a GIF file with a transparent background, as described in Part II.

Use colors that are consistent with the rest of your artwork, but plan on making the background transparent, so that backgrounds of the icons will merge into the background of the page. Adding background colors and effects for the entire page is covered in Part IX.

Often, you will want to create icons with standard symbols, such as arrows, pointing fingers, and computer symbols. Many of these are available as characters in the Windows symbols fonts, such as Wingdings. You can add them to an icon just as we added the two letters in the previous example, without having to do any drawing, simply by changing the font. Call up the Windows "Character Map" utility (found under the Accessories item in the Windows 95 Startup menu) and examine what's available, and you might be surprised.

Creating Horizontal Rules

Narrow horizontal lines (called *rules* from the printing term) are often used on Web pages to separate page elements. There is an HTML command that creates such lines automatically. (In fact, it is the only design element built into HTML.) But such lines are just lines and add no appeal to the page. Also, you might want custom lines to match the overall graphical theme you're trying to achieve.

Keep in mind that such lines are generally about 600 pixels wide, and only a few high. We'll make ours 20 pixels high. (The logo would be hard to recognize if we got any smaller.)

Horizontal rules are of various lengths for various purposes. After some experimenting, you may decide to make yours longer or shorter.

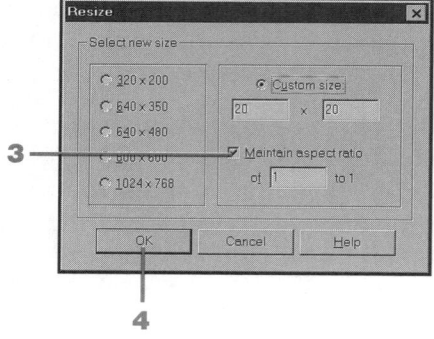

1 Call up the file using the File and the Open commands.

2 Now we'll reduce it in size. Select the Image and then the Resize comands.

3 The Resize dialog window appears. Click the Maintain aspect ratio box, and then replace the Height value with the value we want—in this case, 20.

4 Click OK.

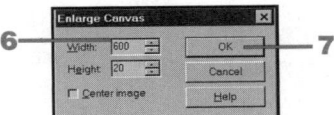

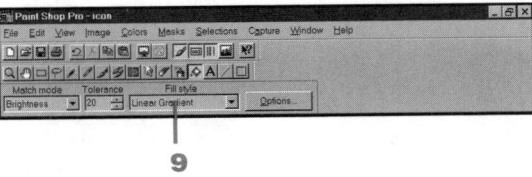

5 Then we turn it into a long line. Select the Image and then the Enlarge Canvas commands.

6 The Enlarge Canvas dialog box appears. Change the Width value to 600. Do not check the Center Image box.

7 Click OK.

8 We're now going to fill in the rest of the horizontal rule using a graphical effect. First, the image has to have a color depth of at least 256 for gray-scale and 16 million for color images. If it does not, select the Colors and then the Increase Color Depth commands, and select either 256 Colors or 16 Million Colors.

9 Select the Flood Fill tool. Several options appear below the tool.

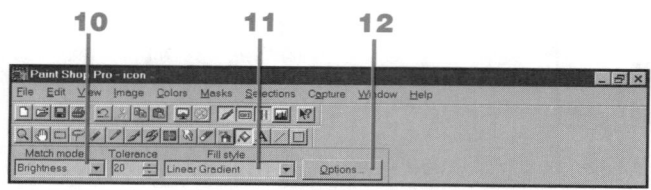

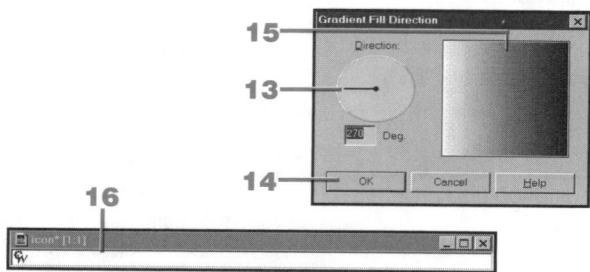

10 Select Brightness for Match Mode.

11 Select Linear Gradient for Fill Style.

12 Several attribute selections appear below it. Click the Options button.

13 You'll see a direction clock indicating which way the pattern will run. You can set the numeric data or move the clock hand. (We used 270 degrees, with the color fading toward the left, so that the icon will still show.)

14 Click OK.

15 Put the Flood Fill cursor inside the work area, and click. The rule will fill in with gray, starting with black at the right, fading to gray at the left, as shown.

16 Save it as a GIF file, as explained in Part II. (Transparency and, for that matter, interlacing, are not concerns.) You now have a custom-made horizontal rule for your Web page.

The other gradient styles—rectangular, sunburst, and radial—are certainly worth experimenting with, especially if you are using color. If you don't like what you see, select the Edit and then the Undo commands, and then try again.

We're assuming the color in use is black. To select some other color to use from within the image, click it with the eyedropper tool before performing the Flood Fill.

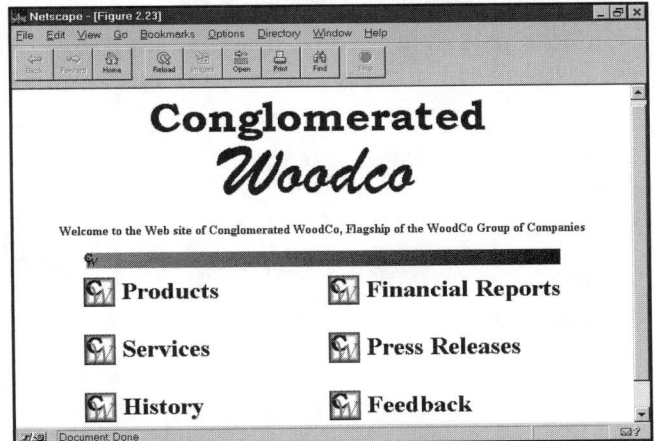

The new horizontal rule in use on a Web page.

Adding Graphics to Your Web Page

Elsewhere, we detailed how to create image files you can use on the Web. In the following sections, we will look at how to use them on the Web.

Using image files on the Web requires that we learn something about the Hypertext Markup Language (HTML), the formatting and Internet navigation language used on the Web.

Standard Web documents—often called Web pages—are files written in HTML. Graphics are embodied in separate files referenced by the code of the HTML document and downloaded to your browser. Your browser software then combines the elements of the page (images and text, for most pages) as specified by the HTML coding, and displays them on your screen within the limits of the available screen sizes, display colors, text fonts, and so on.

So a Web page that uses images actually involves at least two computer files: the image file and the HTML file. The hyperlinks and the formatting commands are embodied in the HTML file. You cannot have a Web page without an HTML file, although you can have a Web page that does not use graphics.

Meanwhile, you can use the name of an image file by itself as the Uniform Resource Locator (URL) for a Web browser. If it is in one of the supported Web graphic formats (GIF, JPG, and PNG), the browser will display the file on the screen, but there will be no hyperlinks or formatting. (If it is not in a supported format, the browser will probably try to start a "helper application" that can display it outside of the browser window.

So, to make use of your images, you must edit HTML files. You should also test them.

HTML is a language you can learn as you go along. Do not be concerned if you don't know it all—you probably don't know every word in the English language, either. Like English, people are out there making up new dialects—which you can learn when the situation arises.

The Editing/Testing Process

HTML files are plain ASCII (what some word processors call text-only) files. Any word processor that can output to ASCII can be used to create and edit an HTML file. (These days some can also output to the HTML format.) However, editing HTML files using full-featured word processors like Microsoft Word or Corel WordPerfect can present a problem, since they do not actually save the revised file until you close the document. (What you are saving in the meantime is a temporary file.) You will have to close and then reopen the document repeatedly while testing it.

Meanwhile, there are perfectly good Web authoring systems that hide the HTML code from you. If you need to occasionally generate an HTML file from scratch, they will help you get through the experience. But it's more typical to be called on periodically to tweak existing HTML files that were manually written by someone else. In such cases, you will need to get at the raw HTML. Fancy tools may just get in the way.

In any event, we'll assume that you have the need and desire to manually edit HTML. In this book, we will assume the use of the Windows Notepad.

Meanwhile, numerous HTML editors are available that specialize in handling, inputting, and editing HTML code. They are often shareware programs and can be downloaded from Web sites that specialize in archiving shareware. But they assume prior knowledge of HTML, and so you cannot expect them to teach you HTML. You should probably try them only after getting your feet wet; then you may find them valuable.

As for testing the files: The beauty of Windows and the like is that you can have more than one program loaded at a time, and flip between them. So you can load your text editor and your browser, edit in one program, and test the file in the other.

It's a fast, painless process. You can be enormously productive. (Or lose yourself tinkering endlessly. The choice is yours.)

Basics of HTML Coding

As mentioned, HTML is plain text. Your browser software interprets it on-the-fly. A basic HTML file may look something like this in its entirety:

```
<HTML>
<HEAD>
<TITLE>Document Name</TITLE>
</HEAD>
<BODY>
All the code for your Web document goes here. Like:
<CENTER><H1>HELLO WORLD!</H1></CENTER>
</BODY>
</HTML>
```

One thing to remember is that HTML is written for machine consumption. The contents could just as easily be strung together in one long line, like this:

```
<HTML><HEAD><TITLE>Document Name</TITLE></HEAD><BODY>All the code for
your Web document goes here. Like:<CENTER><H1>HELLO_WORLD!</H1></CEN-
TER></BODY></HTML>
```

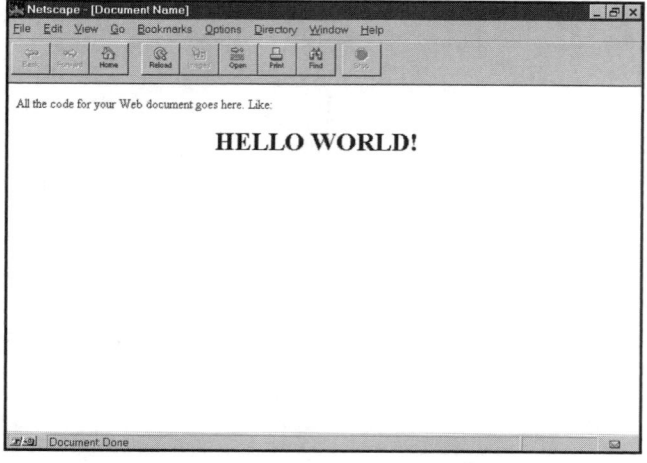

"Hello World!" page produced by the demo HTML file.

But you don't see HTML files that look like that because most were written and edited by human beings, who want to read the material easily. Either way, our code would produce the Web page shown here.

Not only can HTML code be run together without line breaks, but any text you want displayed will additionally be run together without line breaks even if breaks are present in the text. Line breaks in text must be replaced with the HTML **<P>** (paragraph) or **
** (break) function.

Looking at the HTML file itself, you'll notice a lot of arcane text bracketed with the < and the > symbols. These are *tags* and indicate to the browser that the text within the brackets are intended to invoke an HTML formatting function. Learning HTML means learning those functions and the tags that invoke them.

As an example of how they work, note that our "HELLO WORLD!" is centered on the screen in large letters. And you'll note that our HTML file contains the line:

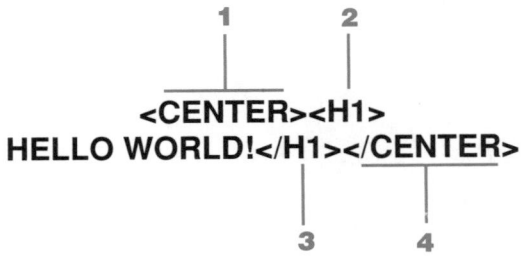

1 <CENTER> turns on the function that centers the text that follows.

2 <H1> turns on the function that renders the following text in the preset Heading 1 format.

3 </H1> turns off the heading format.

4 </CENTER> turns off the centering.

All HTML functions begin with a **<**>** tag and are usually followed by a **</**>** tag, as with **<H1> Hello World!</H1>**.

In our example, you'll note that the text **All the code for your Web document goes here. Like:** is displayed on the page. That is because it was not encased in a tag, and was therefore treated as text. Since no formatting functions had been invoked, it was displayed left-justified in the default font.

Creating a Basic HTML File

As stated, an HTML file is just text with tags. However, certain tags must also be present—at the beginning and at the end of the file—for the file to be an HTML file. What goes between them is where the artistry comes in.

To create your own HTML file, do the following:

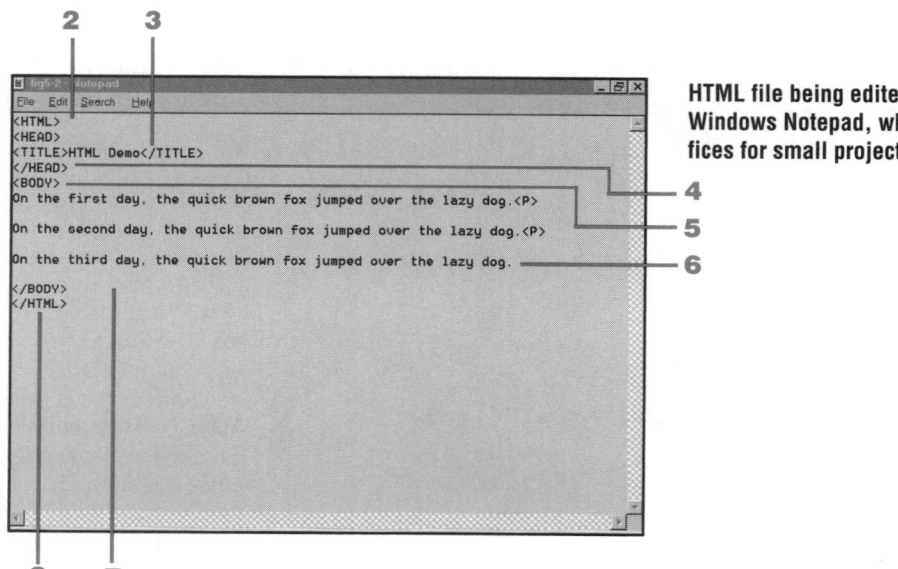

HTML file being edited using Windows Notepad, which suffices for small projects.

1 Launch Notepad or your word processor and begin a new file.

2 Type <HTML>, press Enter to create a new line, and then type <HEAD>.

3 Press Enter and type <TITLE>Document Name</TITLE>.

4 Press Enter and type </HEAD>.

5 Press Enter and type <BODY>.

6 Press Enter and type in whatever you want to say. Remember to put in the <P> tag if you want a paragraph break.

7 Press Enter and type </BODY>.

8 Press Enter and type </HTML>.

9 Save the file using the .htm file extension. In some word processors, you may have to specify that this is to be an ASCII text-only file. (This is not necessary in Notepad.)

10 Now test the file. Launch your browser without going online and load the file you just saved. If you used the text we used, your browser page should look like this.

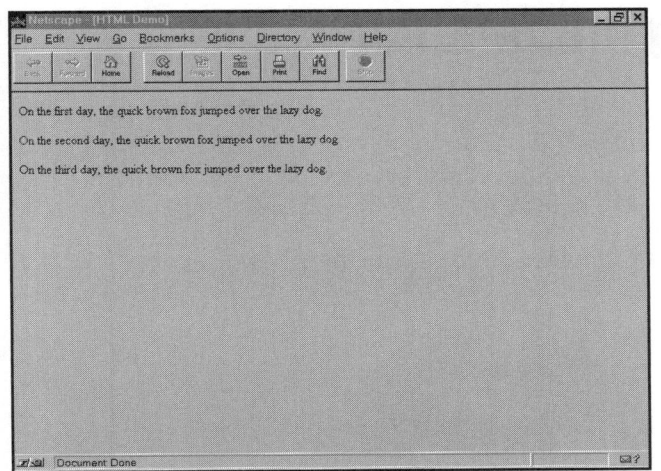

The example file that our code generated.

Remember, you're dealing with a machine. Tiny typos and omissions can lead to nonsensical results. That is why you always have to test your files. With experience, you'll get a feel for what kinds of errors result from what kinds of typos.

Understanding the *IMG* Function

You make images appear in a Web file by using an HTML code command called the **IMG** function. The **IMG** function tells the browser which image to display, and where and how to display it. Additionally, you can describe numerous attributes for the image using the **IMG** function.

A basic HTML file that simply displays an image, using no special attributes, would look like this:

```
<HTML>
<HEAD><TITLE>Document Name</TITLE></HEAD>
<BODY>
<IMG SRC="logo.gif">
</BODY>
</HTML>
```

So the operative HTML function tag is **<IMG SRC="logo.gif">**. The results would look like this:

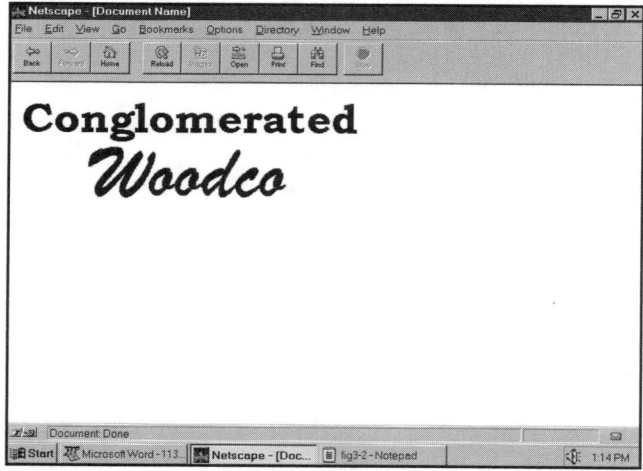

The results of using a simple file with the <IMG SRC="logo.gif"> tag. The image could have been centered horizontally if the IMG tag had been bracketed by <CENTER> and </CENTER> tags.

As you probably surmised, **IMG** stands for "image" and **SRC** stands for "source." Meanwhile, logo.gif is the name of the image file, and it has to be in quotation marks. Since the name, in this case, does not include a file path, the computer assumes that logo.gif is in the same directory. However, a full path name could be used, such as "/pub/stuff/picture.gif."

For that matter, the name could be a full URL and could look like **http://www.anysite.com/picture.gif**. Your Web page could, in theory, make use of any image file stored anywhere on the Web, be it in Finland or Singapore, as long as you know its URL.

While it is possible to do so, it is considered poor practice to link to material on other people's sites without their permission. They can catch you by using a search engine to look for references to their file name.

Adding an Image to an HTML File

So the time has come to create a Web page with an image. We'll assume you have available the simple HTML file created earlier, and an image in the GIF or JPEG format. To add an image to an HTML file, do the following:

1. Establish the name and file path of the image file you want to use. If it is in the same subdirectory as the HTML file, you will need only the name.

2. Open your HTML document, in Notepad or any word processor you would like. (In some word processors, you may have to specify that this is an ASCII text-only file.)

3. Locate the **\<BODY\>** tag.

4. Below the **\<BODY\>** tag but above the **\<BODY\>** tag, insert a blank line.

5. In the blank line, type **\<IMG SRC="path/name of image"\>**.

6. Save the file using the .htm extension. (In some word processors, you may need to close it as well.)

7. Now test the file. Launch your browser without going online and load the file you just saved.

What you see will hopefully match our example, although you'll use your own image with its own dimensions perhaps much different from ours.

Understanding Image Attributes

The **IMG** can also control how the picture is presented, how it is formatted in relation to the other elements on the page, and even how it is used by the server. That's because other items, called attributes, can be added between the **<** and **>** of the **IMG** tag besides **IMG**, **SRC**, and the file name/address. Used together, they can be quite powerful. Table 3.1 presents an overview of the main ones and what they do. (There are other little-used ones that involve proprietary browsers or belong to proposed extensions of HTML.)

Table 3.1 *IMG* Element Attributes

Attribute	Format	Description
ALT	<IMG SRC="any.gif" ALT="text">	Text you want to appear when no image is displayed in the browser.
BORDER	<IMG SRC="any.gif" BORDER="3">	Sets image border thickness (measured in pixels).
ALIGN	<IMG SRC="any.gif" ALIGN=top>	Aligns to the top, middle, or bottom of the text the image is in line with.
HEIGHT	<IMG SRC="any.gif" HEIGHT="3">	Sets the vertical dimension of the image within the browser window.
WIDTH	<IMG SRC="any.gif" WIDTH="3">	Sets the horizontal dimension of the image within the browser window.
LOWSRC	<IMG SRC="a.jpg" LOWSRC="b.gif">	Allows a low-resolution version of an image to be downloaded prior to a high-resolution version, speeding interaction.
VSPACE	<IMG SRC="any.gif" VSPACE="8">	Adds vertical space before and after the image.
HSPACE	<IMG SRC="any.gif" HSPACE="8">	Adds horizontal space before and after the image.
ISMAP	<IMG SRC="any.gif" ISMAP>	For clickable image maps.
USEMAP	<IMG SRC="a.gif" USEMAP="a.map">	Associated with ISMAP.

The attributes can actually go anywhere in the **IMG** tag after the letters **IMG**. For instance, the **ALT** tag in the table could also read **<IMG ALT="text" SRC="any.gif">**. And feel free to write lengthy mega-tags that use every attribute available. The computer wońt complain—it's just a machine.

Finally, you can combine all the attributes you think you need. If a mega-tag like **<IMG SCR="a.jpg" LOWSCR="b.gif" HEIGHT=150 WIDTH=450 BORDER=1 ALIGN=TOP ALT="Click Here To See 2 Fish I Caught">** works for you, then use it. The computer will not balk—it's just a machine.

The ISMAP and **USEMAP** attributes require special treatment, which we'll give them in Part VIII. The other attributes and their effects will be explored as follows.

Adding Alternate Text

The **ALT** (Alternate Text) attribute is used to define what text is to be displayed when the browser is not using graphics. Why?

- Some browsers are non-graphical.

- Some users of graphical browsers turn off the graphics display mode to speed up their Web surfing.

- Some users are vision-impaired, and depend on text-to-speech devices.

In all three cases, the only information available to the users about your image is embodied in whatever text is contained in the **ALT** attribute. So it is common courtesy to put something there, such as a short caption or Click here for link X.

To add an **ALT** attribute to an image, do the following:

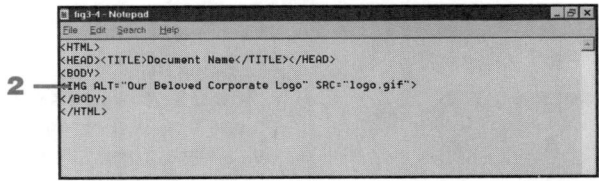

1. Open the HTML document that contains an ALT, in Notepad or any word processor you would like.

2. Locate the IMG tag for the image in question.

3. Inside it, type ALT=*"Your alternate text."*.

4. Save the file using the .htm extension. (In some word processors, you may need to close it as well.)

5. Now test the file. Launch your browser without going online and load the file you just saved. Locate the feature that turns off the display of graphic images, and load the HTML file you just created.

Adding Image Borders

Using the **BORDER** attribute, you can make an image stand out by adding a border to its perimeter. The border's width is measured in pixels.

Setting **BORDER** to 0 will eliminate the highlight border that otherwise surrounds an image that is being used as a link.

To add a **BORDER** attribute to an image, do the following:

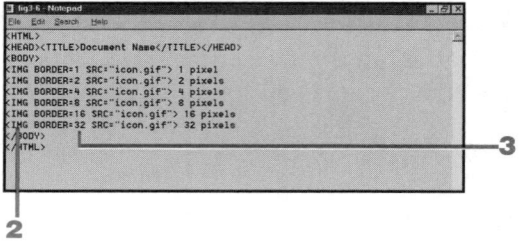

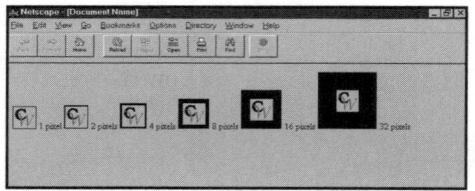

1 Open the HTML document that contains a BORDER attributeit, in Notepad or any word processor you would like.

2 Locate the IMG tag for the image in question.

3 Inside it, type BORDER=*XX* where XX equals the border width you want to use, in pixels.

4 Save the file using the .htm extension. (In some word processors you may need to close it as well.)

5 Now test the file. Launch your browser without going online and load the file you just saved.

It is possible to set the color used by the **BORDER** attribute, as will be discussed in Part IX.

Adjusting Image Alignments

Images and text are often used side-by-side. But how they are actually placed has a great deal to say about the final look of your page. So it's nice to have maximum control over how the browser will perform this task

When deciding what attribute you need to use, remember that it is the image that aligns itself with the text. The placement of the lines of text remains fixed, although lines may be skipped to make room for an image. Table 3.2 shows **ALIGN** attribute options.

Table 3.2 *ALIGN* Attribute Options

Option	Format	Description
TOP	<IMG SRC="a.gif" ALIGN=TOP>	Aligns the top of the image with the approximate top of the text.
MIDDLE	<IMG SRC="a.gif"" ALIGN=MIDDLE>	Aligns the middle of the image with the bottom of the text.
BOTTOM	<IMG SRC="a.gif ALIGN=BOTTOM>	Aligns the bottom of the image with the baseline of the text. (Note that the g, y, j, q, and p descend below the baseline.) BOTTOM is the default value when no ALIGN option is used.
LEFT	<IMG SRC="a.gif" ALIGN=LEFT>	Places the image to the left of the text.
RIGHT	<IMG SRC="a.gif" ALIGN=RIGHT>	Places the image to the right of the text.
TEXTTOP	<IMG SRC="a.gif" ALIGN=TEXTOP>	Aligns the top of the image with the top of the tallest character in the text.
ABSMIDDLE	<IMG SRC="a.gif" ALIGN=ABSMIDDLE>	Aligns the center of the image with the center of the text.
BASELINE	<IMG SRC="a.gif" ALIGN=BASELINE>	Similar to BOTTOM.
ABSBOTTOM	<IMG SRC="a.gif" ALIGN=ABSBOTTOM>	Similar to BOTTOM except that the bottom of the image aligns with the lower descenders of the text.

Text affected by the **ALIGN** option does not wrap. For instance, text using the **TOP** alignment will align with the top of the image—until the end of the line. The text will then wrap to the next text line below the image. With the **BOTTOM** option this looks natural, but with other alignments you will want to use text too short to wrap.

Common sense dictates that you should use overly fancy formatting only when you have a captive audience, such as on a corporate intranet, where the browser software and screen attributes of each user stands a better chance of being known and fixed.

To add an **ALIGN** attribute to an image, do the following:

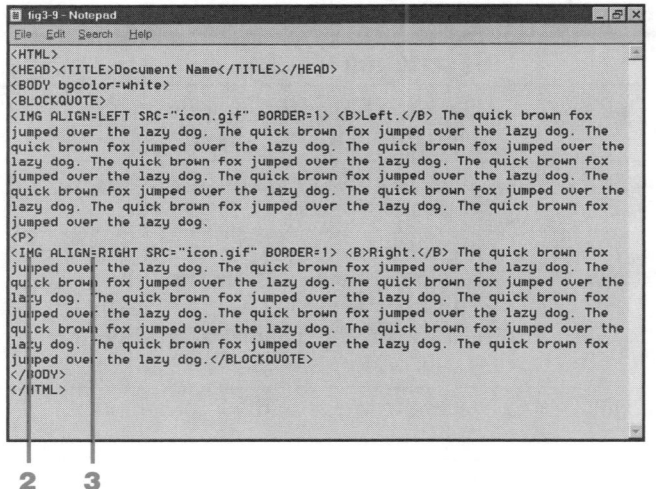

1 Open the HTML document that contains it, in Notepad or any word processor you would like. (In some word processors, you may have to specify that this is an ASCII file.)

2 Locate the IMG tag for the image in question.

3 Inside it, type ALIGN=*X* where X is the alignment you want to use.

4 Save the file using the .htm extension. (In some word processors, you may need to close it as well.)

5 Now test the file. Launch your browser without going online and load the file you just saved.

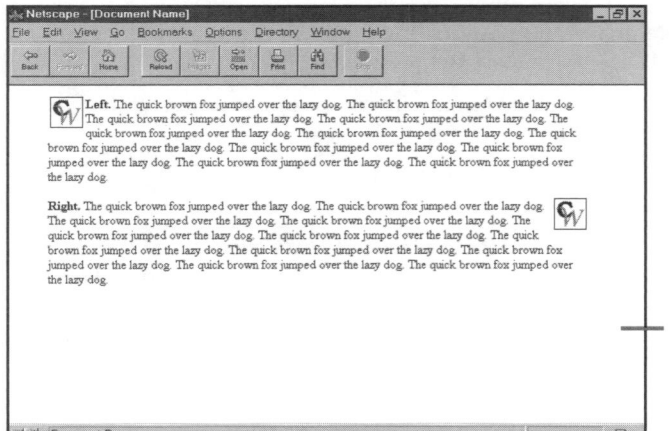

78

Note that the names of the **ALIGN** options can be confusing. For instance, while **TOP** causes the top of the image to align with the top of the text, **MIDDLE** aligns the middle of the image with the baseline of the text, and **BOTTOM** causes the bottom of the image to align with the bottom of the text.

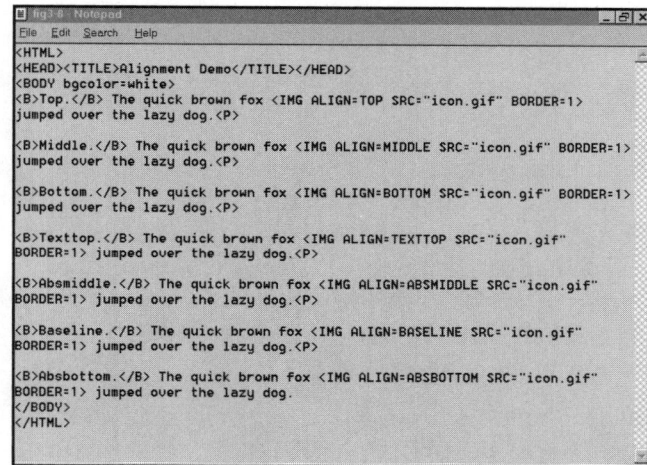

HTML coding for the ALIGN **demonstration, showing the alignment values except** RIGHT **and** LEFT. **The** BORDER **attribute was added for visual clarity.**

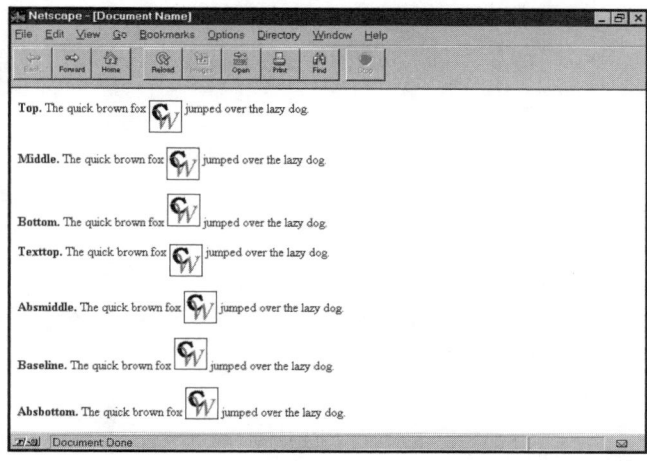

The ALIGN **options except** LEFT **and** RIGHT. **Note that the images align themselves with the text, not vice versa.**

Setting Image Sizes

The HTML **IMG** tag also allows the **HEIGHT** and **WIDTH** attributes, which inform the browser the size of the image in pixels. Of course, even without the **HEIGHT** and **WIDTH** attributes, the browser will figure out the size of your image and lay out the page accordingly. Strictly speaking, you don't need these attributes, (unless you want to resize the image, as explained in the next section). But if you are concerned with making your page download efficiently, you'll want to use these attributes.

By using **HEIGHT** and **WIDTH**, the software can know the size of the image before it receives the image. Therefore, it can leave a blank place on the page for the image and begin filling in text and other elements around it. The browser will not have to reformat the screen after the image finally arrives. But more importantly, the user may begin interacting with the page long before all its elements arrive. And so, by using **HEIGHT** and **WIDTH**, you'll have made the life of a user with a slow connection a little more bearable.

These two browser pages show the difference. On a busy page dominated by a large, high-resolution image, the use of **HEIGHT** and **WIDTH** can make a considerable difference in user satisfaction.

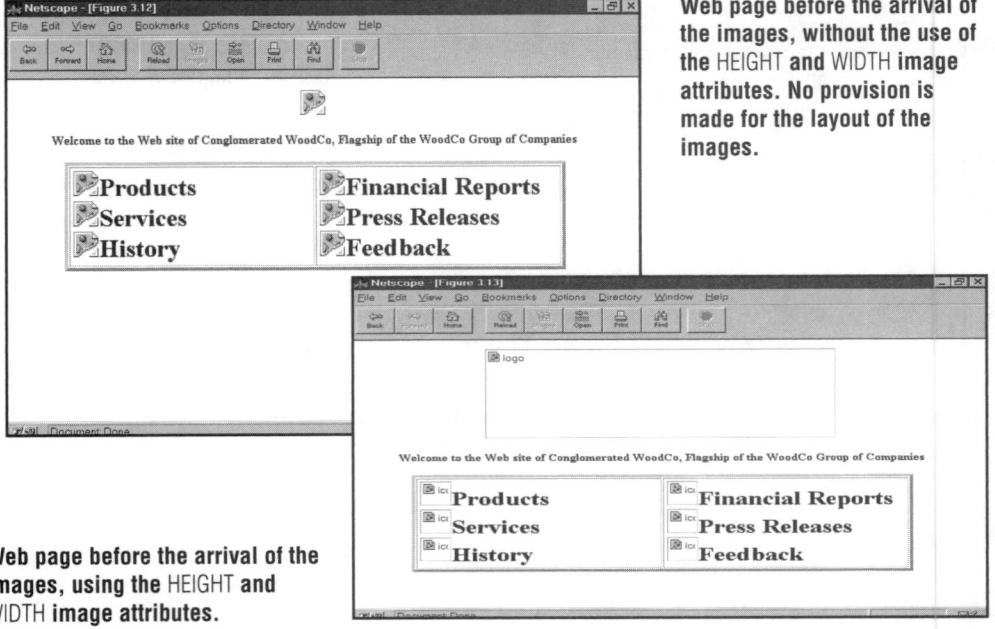

Web page before the arrival of the images, without the use of the HEIGHT and WIDTH image attributes. No provision is made for the layout of the images.

Web page before the arrival of the images, using the HEIGHT and WIDTH image attributes.

To add **HEIGHT** and **WIDTH** attributes to an image, do the following:

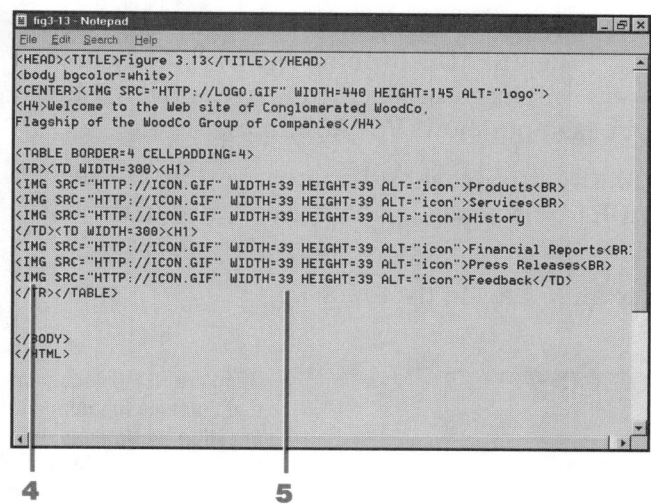

```
fig3-13 - Notepad
File  Edit  Search  Help
<HEAD><TITLE>Figure 3.13</TITLE></HEAD>
<body bgcolor=white>
<CENTER><IMG SRC="HTTP://LOGO.GIF" WIDTH=440 HEIGHT=145 ALT="logo">
<H4>Welcome to the Web site of Conglomerated WoodCo,
Flagship of the WoodCo Group of Companies</H4>

<TABLE BORDER=4 CELLPADDING=4>
<TR><TD WIDTH=300><H1>
<IMG SRC="HTTP://ICON.GIF" WIDTH=39 HEIGHT=39 ALT="icon">Products<BR>
<IMG SRC="HTTP://ICON.GIF" WIDTH=39 HEIGHT=39 ALT="icon">Services<BR>
<IMG SRC="HTTP://ICON.GIF" WIDTH=39 HEIGHT=39 ALT="icon">History
</TD><TD WIDTH=300><H1>
<IMG SRC="HTTP://ICON.GIF" WIDTH=39 HEIGHT=39 ALT="icon">Financial Reports<BR
<IMG SRC="HTTP://ICON.GIF" WIDTH=39 HEIGHT=39 ALT="icon">Press Releases<BR>
<IMG SRC="HTTP://ICON.GIF" WIDTH=39 HEIGHT=39 ALT="icon">Feedback</TD>
</TR></TABLE>


</BODY>
</HTML>
```

4   **5**

1 Examine the image using your graphics software to determine its size in pixels. (In Paint Shop Pro, you can bring up the image's file information readout by selecting the View and then Image Information commands.)

2 Make note of the image's height and width.

3 Open the HTML document that contains the image, in Notepad or any word processor you would like. (In some word processors, you may have to specify that this is an ASCII file.)

4 Locate the IMG tag for the image in question.

5 Inside it, type WIDTH=X and HEIGHT=, where X is the image's width and Y is its height in pixels.

6 Save the file using the .htm extension. (In some word processors, you may need to close it as well.)

7 Now test the file. Launch your browser without going online and load the file you just saved.

81

Adjusting Vertical Spacing

As you lay out a page, you may find yourself trying to separate the images from one another, or images from text. The **VSPACE** attribute lets you specify how much vertical spacing the browser will insert between an image and anything directly above and below it. Our example shows **VSPACE** in use.

When **VSPACE** is in use, the **ALIGN** attribute uses the top or bottom created with the addition of the **VSPACE** pixels, and it is no longer aligned to the borders of the image itself.

To add the **VSPACE** attribute to an image, do the following:

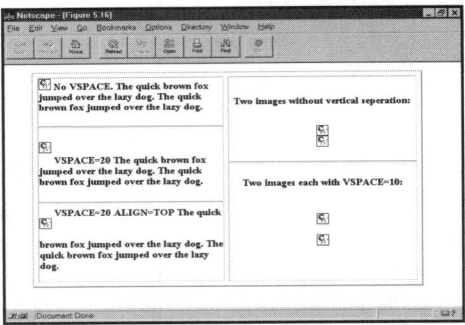

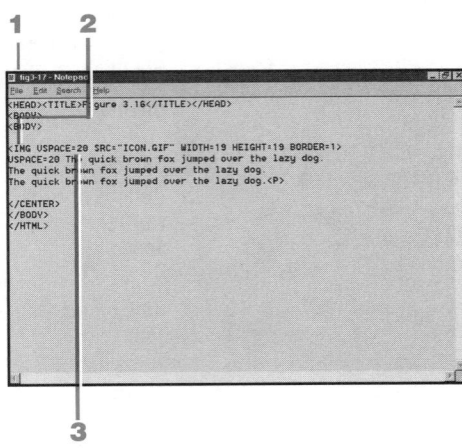

1 Open the HTML document that contains the image in question, in Notepad or any word processor you would like. (In some word processors, you may have to specify that this is an ASCII text-only file.)

2 Locate the IMG tag for the image in question.

3 Inside it, type VSPACE=*X* where X is the spacing you want inserted above and below the image, in pixels.

4 Save the file using the .htm extension. (In some word processors, you may need to close it as well.)

5 Now test the file. Launch your browser without going online and load the file you just saved.

82

Adjusting Horizontal Spacing

As you lay out a page, you may find yourself trying to horizontally separate the images from one another, or images from text. The **HSPACE** attribute puts space (measured in pixels) to the right and left of the image. Unlike **HSPACE**—which inserts vertical spacing—text alignment is usually not an issue. Our example shows **HSPACE** in use.

Text alignment is not complicated by **HSPACE**, but note that **HSPACE** will cause the image to be indented from the text margin.

To add the **HSPACE** attribute to an image, do the following:

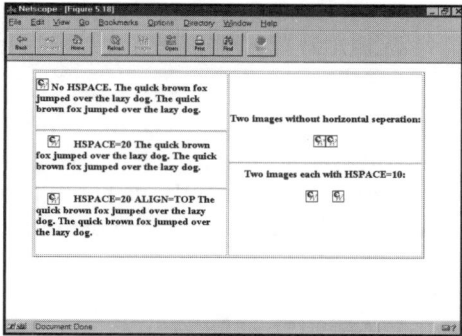

1 Open the HTML document that contains the image in question, in Notepad or any word processor you would like. (In some word processors, you may have to specify that this is an ASCII text-only file.)

2 Locate the IMG tag for the image in question.

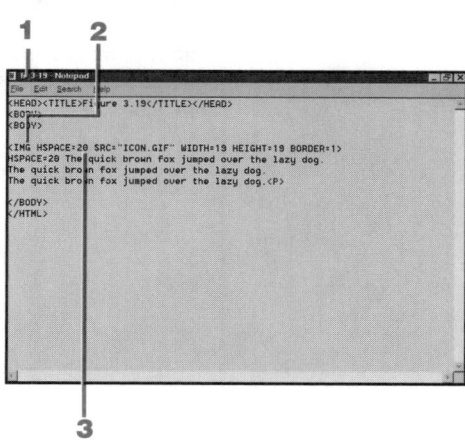

3 Inside it, type HSPACE=*X* where X is the spacing you want inserted to the right and left of the image, in pixels.

4 Save the file using the .htm extension. (In some word processors, you may need to close it as well.)

5 Now test the file. Launch your browser without going online and load the file you just saved.

Using Low-Resolution Stand-Ins

When you are committed to using large, high-resolution images but want to remain accessible to all users, an attribute you might use is **LOWSRC**. Basically, it lets you specify two images in an **IMG** tag:

- The first is the **LOWSRC** (low-resolution source) that will be loaded by the browser on the first pass as it lays out the page.

- The second is the standard and presumably high-resolution **SRC** (source image) of the **IMG** tag, which the browser will load on the second pass.

Therefore, the user will have a full screen with some kind of recognizable image to interact with long before the full high-resolution arrives. **LOWSRC** is especially useful when you want to use clickable image maps: You can create a sort of first pass with the basic options visible, and then fill in the scenery in the second pass.

It is unlikely that your **LOWSRC** image will have the same colors or resolution as the final high-resolution **SRC** image, and sometimes might not have the same dimensions, but that is not really a concern. All you have to do is include **HEIGHT** and **WIDTH** attributes in the **IMG** tag that match the measurements of the high-resolution image, and the low-resolution image will be resized to match. (Or, if neither of their sizes matches, both images will be resized.)

The process begins: The initial LOWSRC image is displayed, in this case an enormously resized version of our corporate icon.

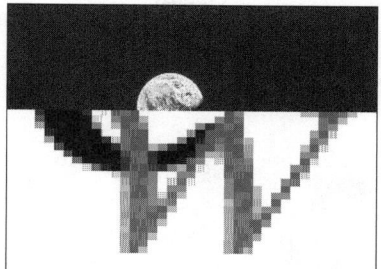

Second stage: The SRC (high-resolution) image is being loaded over the original LOWSRC **image.**

Final stage: The high-resolution SRC image is loaded into the space formerly occupied by the LOWSRC **image.**

Traditionally, a JPG file is the **SRC** and a GIF file is the **LOWSRC** image, but you can use either or both formats (and, presumably in the future, PNG).

To add the **LOWSRC** attribute to an image, do the following:

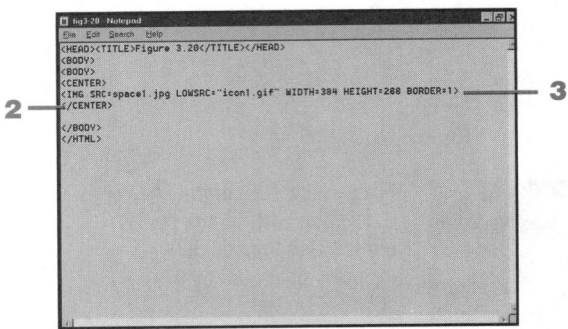

1 Open the HTML document that uses the image in question, in Notepad or any word processor you would like. (In some word processors, you may have to specify that this is an ASCII text-only file.)

2 Locate the IMG tag for the image in question.

3 Inside it, type LOWSRC=X where X is the name for the low-resolution file that will stand in for the final file (which is named by the "SRC=" attribute.) Also type in HEIGHT=Y and WIDTH=Z where Y and Z are the dimensions of the final high-resolution files, noted earlier.

4 Save the file using the .htm extension. (In some word processors, you may need to close it as well.)

5 Now test the file. Launch your browser without going online and load the file you just saved.

At this writing, **LOWSRC** is supported by Netscape Navigator. Internet Explorer ignores the **LOWSRC** image and displays only the **SRC** image.

Adding Text to Web Files

You will, of course, want to add text to your pages—most images are a little bland without text. For that you need to learn some HTML. This book will not attempt to teach you the whole world of HTML. There are weighty tomes that do that. It *will* show you how to perform some basic tasks, with minimal grief.

But after learning the basics of HTML, you can then press on, experiment, and soon feel at home in the medium. Remember, reading a book on playing the piano and the notes it produces will not teach you to play. You have to sit at the keyboard for a time. Later, we will teach you some tags and a few lines of HTML. It is up to you to sit at the keyboard and use them.

The following code is a functional, self-contained HTML file that displays three sentences:

```
<HTML><HEAD><TITLE>Figure 3.25</TITLE></HEAD><BODY
<BODY>
The quick brown fox jumped over the lazy dog.
The quick brown fox jumped over the lazy dog.
The quick brown fox jumped over the lazy dog.
</BODY>
</HTML>
```

If you've read Part V, you understand what **<>** tags are. In our example we have the document description tags that every HTML file begins and ends with. And between those tags we have text. The browser will simply display the text, using its default font and colors, as shown in this figure.

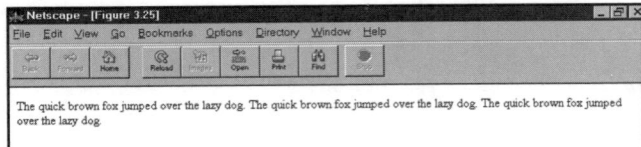

These three sentences were originally on three separate lines—the browser runs them together because HTML uses its own end-of-paragraph markers.

Right away you'll notice the main problem confronted when dealing with text in HTML. HTML does not recognize the end-of-line markers used by ASCII or, for that manner, any other word processor. As a result, the three sentences are jammed together as one, on one line.

When transferring text to HTML, you have to add your own end-of-line markers. For the end of the paragraph, you add the **<P>** tag. It adds a line break, plus a small amount of inter-paragraph spacing. For a line break without the paragraph spacing, you use the **
** tag. The idea is expanded with the following examples:

<HTML><HEAD><TITLE>Line Break Demo</TITLE></HEAD><BODY>
The quick brown fox jumped over the lazy dog.<P>
The quick brown fox jumped over the lazy dog.<P>
**The quick brown fox jumped over the lazy dog.
**
**The quick brown fox jumped over the lazy dog.
**
</BODY>
</HTML>

The **<P>** tag can be at the start or end of a paragraph—the effect is the same. Some purists put a **<P>** at the start and a **</P>** at the end of paragraphs, but this is not required by the browsers.

Text will be displayed with its original line breaks intact if you format it with the **<PRE>** tag, which is explained later. But using **<PRE>** limits the other formatting you can do, and you may be better off pretending it does not exist.

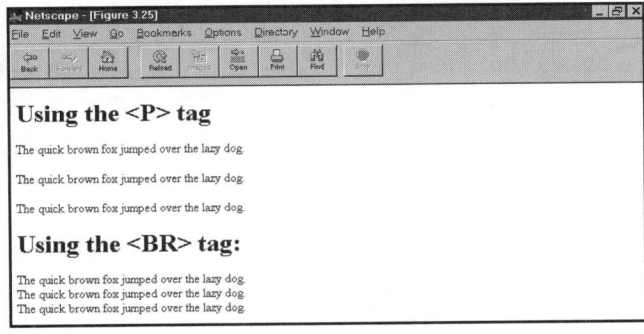

Effect of using the <P> end-of-paragraph and <BR> line-break tags in HTML. The <P> adds extra paragraph spacing.

The upshot is that you cannot just cut and paste text from a word processing document into an HTML file. First, you have to account for the end-of-line markers. The actual details of how you do this will vary from word processor to word processor, but the following should give you the general idea:

1 Open a file in a word processor, or Windows Notepad, in the ASCII text-only format. (Notepad is in ASCII format to begin with.)

2 Add the document description tags. At the top you can type in "<HTML><HEAD><TITLE> your title here </TITLE><HEAD><BODY>." Then press Enter and type </BODY></HTML>. ("your title here", of course, can be anything you want.)

3 Launch your word processor and then cut and paste the text you want to use into a new, separate working document.

4 In the new document, use the search/replace function to locate each end-of-paragraph marker and replace it with a combined <P> tag and carriage return. (You should eliminate the carriage return and leave just the <P> tag, but leaving the carriage return makes the text more legible. HTML will ignore the carriage returns anyway.)

5 Cut the text in the working document.

6 Switch to the HTML file you created earlier.

7 Put the cursor in the blank line between the document-description start and end tags.

8 Paste the text.

9 Save the file, using an appropriate name and the .htm extension. (In some word processors you may have to close the file as well.)

10 Now test the file. Launch your browser without going online, and load the file you just created by choosing the appropriate File Open command, and then browsing to find the file.

Changing the Appearance of Text

Merely cutting and pasting text from your word processor into an HTML file will lead to disappointing results. In your word processor, you were able to make selected text **boldfaced**, *italic*, <u>underlined</u>, an so forth. After cutting and pasting text into an ASCII format HTML file, those attributes disappear and only raw text is displayed.

However, there are HTML tags to add many of these attributes to an HTML document. Table 6.3 lays out the tags you are likely to encounter.

Table 6.3 Tags for Changing Text Appearance

Element	Description	Format
SMALL	Smaller font	`<SMALL>Text</SMALL>`
BIG	Larger font	`<BIG>Text</BIG>`
B	Boldfaced	`<B>Text</B>`
I	Italic	`<I>Text</I>`
S	Strikethrough	`<S>Text</S>`
U	Underline	`<U>Text</U>`
SUB	Subscript	`<SUB>Text</SUB>`
SUP	Superscript	`<SUP>Text</SUP>`
TT	Typewriter-style font	`<TT>Text</TT>`
EM	Emphasis	`<EM>Text</EM>`
STRONG	Strong emphasis	`<STRONG>Text</STRONG>`
SAMP	Sample code	`<SAMP>Text</SAMP>`
CODE	Sample code	`<CODE>Text</CODE>`
KBD	Keyboard input prompt	`<KBD>Text</KBD>`
VAR	Program variable	`<VAR>Text</VAR>`
DFN	Definition	`<DFN>Text</DFN>`
CITE	Citation	`<CITE>Text</CITE>`
ADDRESS	Address	`<ADDRESS>Text</ADDRESS>`

The next figure shows examples of the tags in use. Notice that after the **TT** tag nothing new is produced by the rest of the tags—the tags just produce italic, bold, default, or monospace (as on a typewriter) output. This is due to the fact that it is up to the browser to set the display mode for each tag. The way certain tags—bold, italic, and so forth—should be displayed is obvious, and they are heavily used. Other tags, while part of the HTML specifications, are rarely used and not fully supported. They remain part of the specification, though, for special-purpose use.

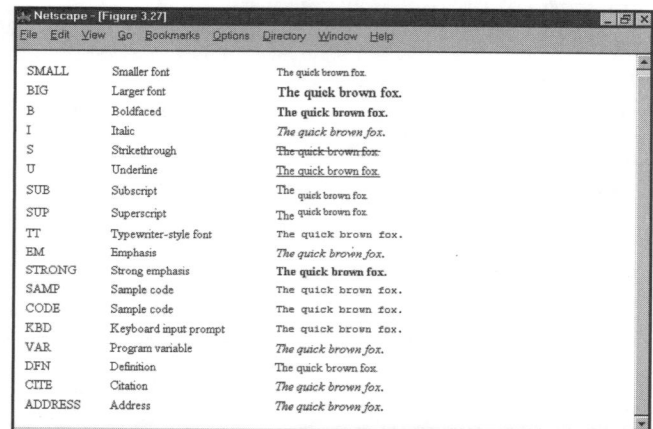

The effect of HTML text-appearance tags. The actual appearance of the text is determined by the browser software, which in this case is Netscape Navigator. The lesser-used tags (after TT) are for special purposes and have no special format.

The same HTML file, rendered by Microsoft Internet Explorer. Aside from using a different default font, there are differences in the way that some lesser-used tags are represented.

Remember, on the Internet, you relinquish total control over the appearance of your material on the users' screens. For the sake of simplicity, you might want to restrict yourself to using bold, italic, and underline.

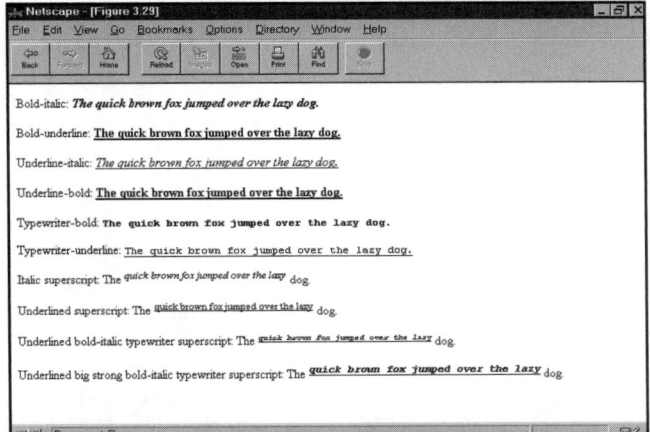

Samples of combined appearance tags rendered by Netscape Navigator.

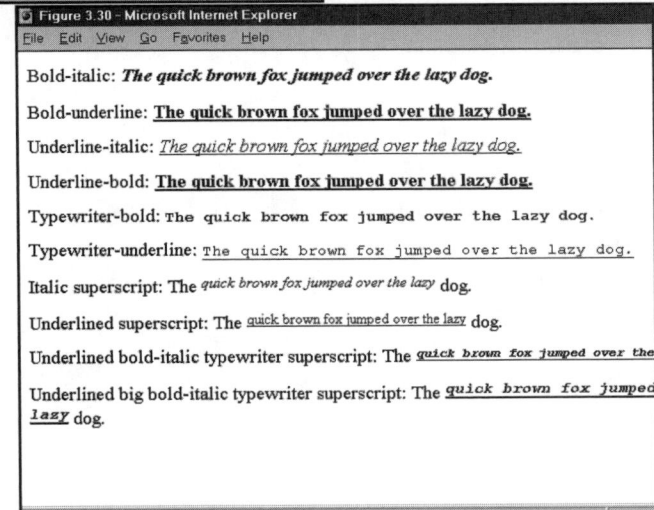

Samples of combined appearance tags rendered by Microsoft Internet Explorer.

It is possible to combine multiple tags, and most browsers (especially the latest generation) will support them. Thus, you can produce combinations like bold-italic. Again, the results are not entirely predictable on all browsers, and you may want to forego anything too fancy.

To add text-appearance tags to text in an HTML file, do the following:

The quick brown fox jumped over the lazy dog.

\<B>The quick \<I>brown fox jumped over \<B>the lazy \<U>dog.

\<B>The\</B> quick \<I>brown\</I> fox jumped over \<B>the\</B> lazy \<U>dog.\</U>

1 Open the HTML file by using either a word processor or Notepad. If it is a word processor, make sure to set it to handle text in the ASCII format.

2 Locate the text whose appearance you want changed.

3 Put the opening tag—such as \<B>, \<I>, or \<U>—at the beginning of the text.

4 Put the end tag—such as \</B>, \</I>, or \</U>—at the end of the text.

5 Save the file, making sure it remains in the ASCII text-only format and retains the .htm extension. (In some word processors, you may have to close the file as well.)

6 Now test the file. Launch your browser without going online and load the file you just saved.

Special-purpose HTML editors are designed to let you add an attribute by first highlighting the text and then clicking a menu option. The tag and end tag are then inserted in the proper place. The benefit is not only ease of use, but also an accurate rendition of what the HTML will look like in a browser.

Changing Text Size

The HTML **<FONT>** tag gives you some measure of control over the size, type-face, and color of the text. In this section, we'll look at using it to change the text size. (Headings, which also change text size, are covered in the Changing Text Format section, since they affect format as well.)

When publishing with ink on paper, you specify text in point sizes. (There are about 72 points in an inch, and the text of most reading material is eight to twelve points high.) Your control over the size, position, and appearance of the text is total.

With Web publishing, you enjoy no such control. You don't know what screen size and resolution are being used by a given user, and if you do, you still don't know what dimensions the browser window has been sized to.

However, you do know that the browser has a default font. Therefore, you can define font sizes in relative terms, relative to the default font. The **<FONT>** tag enables you to set the relative size of the font at values between 1 and 7, where the default size is 3. (Yes, it's arbitrary. The difference between size 1 and size 7 is actually a little more than a factor of 5.)

Keep in mind that **<FONT>** tags derive their font sizes relative to the same default size. So piling **<FONT>** tag atop **<FONT>** tag does not result in bigger screen fonts—each tag produces its same font size, regardless of whatever font size was just used. The next figure shows the **<FONT SIZE>** tag in use.

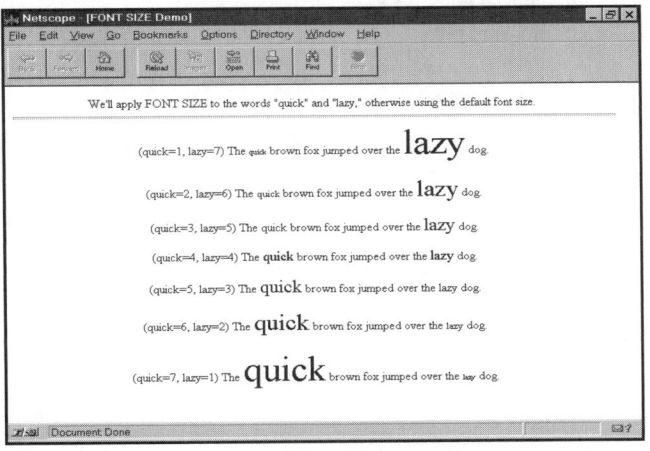

The effect of using the <FONT> tag.

To change the size of some text in an HTML file, do the following.

2

The quick brown fox jumped over the lazy dog.

3

The <FONT SIZE=1>quick brown fox jumped over the <FONT SIZE=7>lazy</FONT> dog.

4

The <FONT SIZE=1>quick</FONT> brown fox jumped over the ➡<FONT SIZE=7>lazy</FONT> dog

1 Open the HTML file by using either a word processor or Notepad. If it is a word processor, make sure to set it to handle text in the ASCII format.

2 Locate the text whose size you want changed.

3 Directly before that text, insert <FONT SIZE=X>, where X is the relative size you want for the text and 3 is the default size of the text. If you want

smaller text, X can be 3, 2, or even 1. If you want a little larger text size, X can be 4 or 5. If you want dramatically larger text, X can be 6 or 7.

4 Locate the end of the text whose size you want changed, and insert the </FONT> end tag.

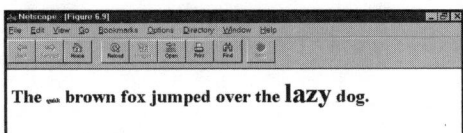

5 Save the file, making sure it remains in the ASCII text-only format and retains the .htm extension. With some word processors, you may have to close the file as well.

6 Now test the file. Launch your browser without going online and load the file you just saved.

7 Examine the resulting page. Does it achieve the effect you sought? Does it throw other elements off? You may have to make several adjustments before you are satisfied.

97

Changing Text Fonts

The HTML **<FONT>** tag gives you some measure of control over the size, typeface, and color of the text. Changing typeface is a simple matter of adding the **FACE** attribute to the **<FONT>** tag. For instance, the following line of code would cause the text starting at the **FACE** tag to appear in a font called Century Gothic:

<FONT FACE="Century Gothic">Hello</FONT>

You must use the name of the font as given by the user's Fonts Control Panel. But you are not sitting at the machine of every possible user and can't know which fonts are available. And if the browser software of a particular user cannot find Century Gothic, then the text will be displayed in the default font. Whatever special impact you were trying to make will be lost on that person. Use of the **FACE** attribute would seem to make the most sense in controlled settings like corporate intranets, where the users should have a uniform configuration.

It is possible to put in a (comma-separated) list of possible fonts, hoping that at least one will show up on the user's machine. Here, we have three possible fonts to assign to the text:

<FONT FACE="Century Gothic", "Bookman Old Style Bold",
➥"Britannic Bold">Hello</FONT>

Notice that the commas are outside the quotation marks. The next figure shows the kind of thing can be done using **FACE**.

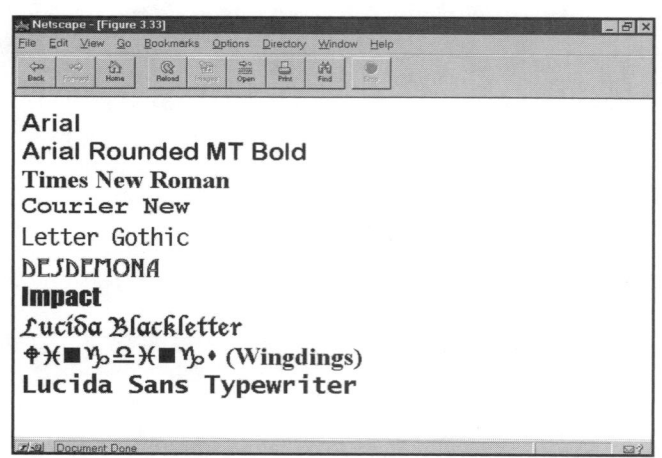

Different fonts displayed using the FACE attribute. Each name is also the name used in the FACE attribute.

Beyond logos, copyright notices, and decorative items, two fonts per page is sufficient: one for the headlines and titles, and the other for the text. To display text in an HTML file in a specific font, do the following.

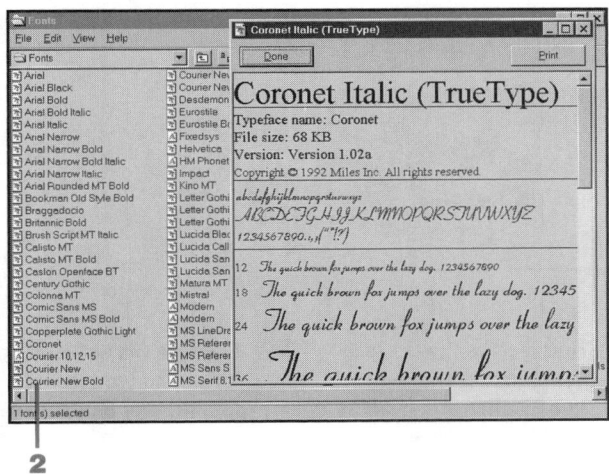

2

4

The quick brown fox jumped over the lazy dog.

5

The \<FONT FACE="Century Gothic", "Bookman Old Style Bold", ➥"Britannic Bold">quick brown fox jumped over the lazy dog.

5

1 Call up your Control Panel and then the Fonts Control Panel.

2 Make a note of the likely font names—fonts you suspect the target users will have. If you are not sure about the appearance of a font, click its icon to bring up a sample screen, as shown.

3 Open the HTML file whose text fonts you want to change, using either a word processor or Notepad. If it is a word processor, make sure to set it to handle text in the ASCII text-only format.

4 Locate the text whose font you want changed.

5 Directly before that text, insert \<FONT FACE= "X"> where X is the name of the font you selected. To increase the chances of naming a font the user will have, you can list more than one, each in quotation marks with a comma between them.

99

The <FONT FACE="Century Gothic", "Bookman Old Style Bold", ➥"Britannic Bold">quick brown fox</FONT> jumped over the lazy dog.

6

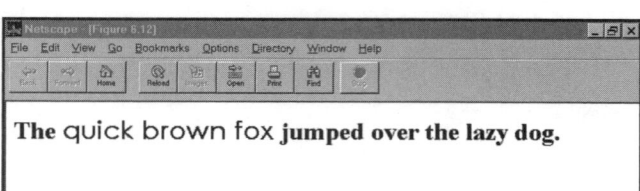

6 Locate the end of the text whose size you want changed, and insert the </FONT> end tag, as shown.

7 Save the file, making sure it remains in the ASCII text-only format and retains the .htm extension. In some word processors, you may have to close the file as well.

8 Now test the file. Launch your browser without going online and load the file you just saved.

9 Examine the resulting page. Does it achieve the effect you sought? Does it throw other elements off?

10 If you are satisfied, repeat the process and replace the font name with XXX. This will force the browser to use the default font.

11 Save the file and examine it with the browser. This is the way that Internet users without the font you named will see the page. If you are still satisfied, then you can proceed in confidence.

Changing Text Colors

The HTML **<FONT>** tag gives you some measure of control over the size, type-face, and color of the text. Now we will look at using the **<FONT>** tag to change the color of the text.

Basically, to change the font color, you add the **COLOR** attribute to the **<FONT>** tag. But remember that you are assuming the user has a color screen and has not set his or her browser to override your document's color selection. Otherwise, the effects you are planning will be lost on this user.

The syntax looks simple:

<FONT COLOR="X">_text_**</FONT>**

However, _X_ can either be the name of a color (placed in quotation marks) or the RGB hexadecimal value for a color.

By "name of a color," we mean a predefined name that the browser supports. Netscape Navigator supports well over 100 predefined color names. Microsoft Internet Explorer supports far fewer. The following list (demonstrated in the next figure) includes most of the colors common to both those browsers:

AQUA	**NAVY**
BLACK	**OLIVE**
BLUE	**PURPLE**
GRAY	**RED**
GREEN	**SILVER**
LIME	**TEAL**
MAROON	**YELLOW**
WHITE	

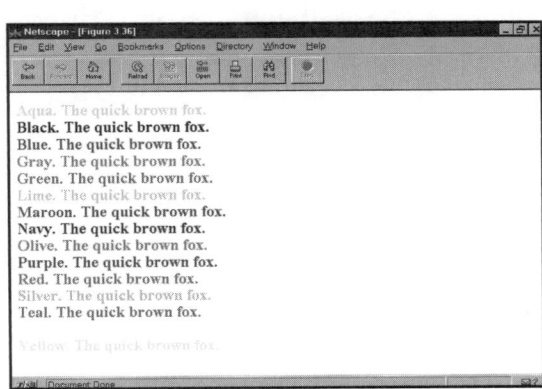

The color list rendered using the <FONT> tag. Here, of course, the colors are shades of gray, and the WHITE entry is lost to the background. Be assured that GREEN, LIME, and OLIVE are different shades and not synonyms; likewise with NAVY, BLUE, and AQUA.

101

So if you think some text ought to be purple, the syntax would be:

<FONT COLOR="PURPLE">text</FONT>

The RGB hexadecimal value is the color broken down into its red, blue, and green components, each of which has a value of 0 to 255. You then render those numbers in the base-16 hexadecimal system, where **A** is the same as 10, **F** is the same as 16, and **FF** is the same as 255. Having determined what those three hexadecimal values are, you then run them together into one six-digit number. The syntax looks like this:

<FONT COLOR="#RRGGBB">text</FONT>

Assume you want to use the color blue. Red and green are not employed and therefore are each **00**. Blue is at its full value of 255, or **FF** in hexadecimal. The resulting syntax looks like this:

<FONT COLOR="#0000FF">text</FONT>

Note that the RRGGBB number must begin with the **#** symbol (which tells the world that this is a hexadecimal number) and the whole number must be in quotation marks.

Obviously, the number of colors you can create is enormous. Yes, you could tinker forever—but there are good reasons to specify your own color rather than choosing from the previous list. For instance, perhaps there's an official corporate scheme you want to emulate. The following table indicates starting points for your color searches.

Table 6.5 RRGGBB Values for Traditional Colors

Color	RRGGBB Value	Color	RRGGBB Value
Black	000000	Purple	FF00FF
White	FFFFFF	Yellow	00FFFF
Red	FF0000	Brown	996633
Green	00FF00	Gray	A0A0A0
Blue	0000FF		

It is possible to set the color of the page's background, and to set the default color of the text. These settings will be discussed in Part IX.

To display text in an HTML file in a specific color, do the following:

1. Determine which color you want to use and see if it is one of the predefined colors. If it is not, determine what its RGB value is.

2. Open the HTML file where you want to change the text color, using either a word processor or Notepad. If it is a word processor, make sure it is set to handle text in the ASCII text-only format.

3. Locate the text for which you want the color changed.

4. Directly before that text, insert **<FONT COLOR="*X*">** where *X* is the name or value of the color you selected.

5. Locate the end of the text for which you want the size changed, and insert the **</FONT>** end tag.

6. Save the file, making sure it remains in the ASCII format and retains the .htm extension. In some word processors, you may have to close the file as well.

7. Now test the file. Launch your browser without going online and load the file you just saved.

You can, of course, combine all three **FONT** attributes in one tag. If you want text that's large, red, and in Arial, use **<FONT COLOR="RED" SIZE=7 FACE="Arial">**.

Changing Text Formats

Previously, we have shown how to format images and text together, and how to control the appearance of text. But predefined formats can be assigned to the text itself to control how it arranges itself on the page.

Again, total control over the final appearance of the layout is not possible. But artful use of the HTML format functions, alone or in combination, will probably produce usable results.

The HTML text layout tags fall into two classifications: formatting and lists. The formatting functions concern headlines and blocks of text. Lists are more complicated and are intended for tabular material, although no rule prevents you from using them to format blocks of text.

The following table details the available formatting functions.

Table 6.6 HTML Text Formatting Functions

Name	Syntax	Comment
BLOCKQUOTE	<BLOCKQUOTE>*text* </BLOCKQUOTE>	Indents both margins.
PREFORMATTED	<PRE>*text*</PRE>	Preserves spacing and line breaks.
LISTING	<LISTING>*text*></LISTING>	Denotes program listings: small-font version of **PREFORMATTED**.
CENTER	<CENTER>*text*</CENTER>	Centers the text on the page.
Heading 1	<H1>*text*</H1>	Largest heading
Heading 2	<H2>*text*</H2>	Second largest heading
Heading 3	<H3>*text*</H3>	Third largest heading
Heading 4	<H4>*text*</H4>	Fourth largest heading
Heading 5	<H5>*text*</H5>	Fifth largest heading
Heading 6	<H6>*text*</H6>	Smallest heading, often smaller than default text. (Not always supported.)

The next figure shows the same functions in use. Note that we have counted the heading styles as formatting functions instead of text appearance functions because the heading end tags force a paragraph break, as do the other format (and list) tags.

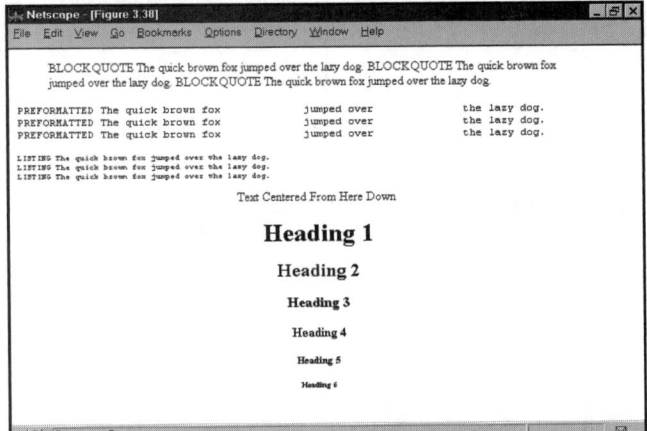

The effect of using the formatting functions shown in the table. BLOCKQUOTE **indents** while PREFORMATTED and LISTING **preserve spacing and line breaks.**

PREFORMATTED and **LISTING** differ from other HTML functions in that any spacing or line breaks in the original text will show up on the screen. Normally, HTML ignores standard line breaks and multiple spaces.

105

To add text formatting functions to an HTML file, do the following.

Note how the formatting tags also trigger line breaks, so that the work "fox," while centered, is on a line by itself.

1 Open the HTML file that you want to edit, using either a word processor or Windows Notepad. If it is a word processor, make sure it is set to handle text in the ASCII text-only format.

2 Locate the text whose format you want to alter.

3 Directly before that text, insert the beginning tag of the function, either <BLOCKQUOTE>, <PREFORMATTED>, <LISTING>, <CENTER>, or a heading tag.

4 Locate the end of the text you want to change, and insert the end tag.

5 Save the file, making sure it remains in the ASCII text-only format and retains the .htm extension. In some word processors, you may have to close the file as well.

6 Now test the file. Launch your browser without going online and load the file you just saved.

Standard HTML formatting produces text in one column. The creation of multiple columns requires the use of the **TABLE** function, which will be discussed along with special effects in Part VII.

Formatting Text as Lists

HTML has several functions for arranging information in lists. These functions require several element tags: the first to start the list, then tags to denote list items, and then the end tag. The **DEFINITION** list differs in that there are two kinds of list items: the "Definition Title" (basically the header) and the "Definition Data" (the list items).

Table 6.7 HTML List Functions with Elements

Type	Syntax

UNORDERED List	`<UL>`
	`<LI>`The Quick Brown Fox
	`<LI>`Jumped Over
	`<LI>`The Lazy Dog
	`</UL>`

ORDERED (numbered) List	`<OL>`
	`<LI>`The Quick Brown Fox
	`<LI>`Jumped Over
	`<LI>`The Lazy Dog
	`</OL>`

MENU List	`<MENU>`
	`<LI>`The Quick Brown Fox
	`<LI>`Jumped Over
	`<LI>`The Lazy Dog
	`</MENU>`

DIRECTORY List	`<DIR>`
	`<LI>`The Quick Brown Fox
	`<LI>`Jumped Over
	`<LI>`The Lazy Dog
	`</DIR>`

DEFINITION List	`<DL>`
	`<DT>`Definition Title
	`<DD>`Definition Data
	`<DD>`Definition Data
	`</DL>`

The next figure shows the lists in actual use. As you can see, the **ORDERED** list adds numbers to the list items, while the **UNORDERED** list just adds bullets. There is no immediate difference between the **UNORDERED**, **MENU**, and **DIRECTORY** lists. The **DEFINITION** list does not indent the first (or "Definition Title") item in the list (to which many people add boldfacing) but does indent the remaining ("Definition Data") items.

With the list formats, lines of text long enough to wrap remain indented. Therefore, you see people using the **DEFINITION** format on standard text to achieve the indentation they want.

The list items tags (**<LI>**, **<DT>**, and **<DD>**) insert line breaks, so there is no need for additional **<P>** or **
** tags at the end of the item lines.

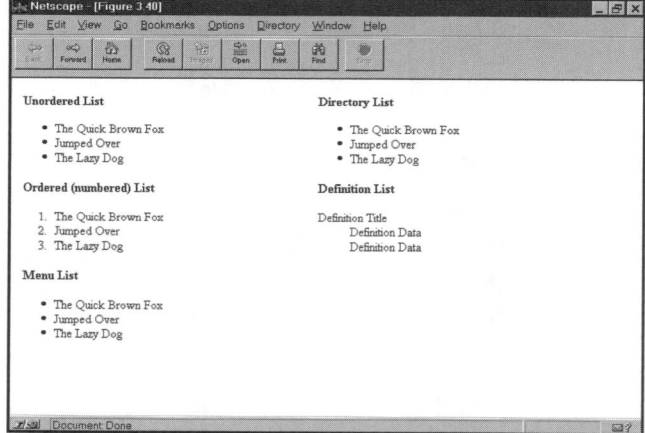

HTML list format in use, with default bullets and numbers. The browser—Netscape Navigator in this case—makes no distinction between UNORDERED, MENU, and DIRECTORY lists.

To format text as a list in an HTML file, do the following.

Fruit:

Apples

Oranges

Bananas

Pears

Fruit:

<UL>

Apples

Oranges

Bananas

Pears

Fruit:

<UL>

<LI>Apples

<LI>Oranges

<LI>Bananas

<LI>Pears

1 Open the HTML file that you want to edit, using either a word processor or Windows Notepad. If it is a word processor, make sure it is set to handle text in the ASCII format.

2 Locate the text that you want to format as a list.

3 Directly before that text (probably on a line by itself for legibility), insert the beginning tag for the style of list you wish to use: either <UL>, <OL>, <MENU>, <DIR>, or <DL>.

4 If you are not using a DEFI-NITION list, before the text of each separate list item, place the <LI> (list item) tag and then skip to Step 7.

5 If you are using a DEFINI-TION list, in front of the text that will serve as the list title or heading, place the <DT> (definition title) tag.

6 In front of each of the rest of the items in the list, place the <DD> (definition data) tag.

\<DL\>

\<DT\>Fruit:

Apples

Oranges

Bananas

Pears

\<DF\>

\<DT\>Fruit:

\<DD\>Apples

\<DD\>Oranges

\<DD\>Bananas

\<DD\>Pears

7 Locate the end of the text that composes the list and place the end tag (probably on a line by itself for legibility); either \</UL\>, \</OL\>, \</MENU\>, \</DIR\>, **or** \</DL\>.

8 Save the file, making sure it remains in the ASCII text-only format and retains the .htm extension. In some word processors, you may have to close the file as well.

9 Now test the file. Launch your browser without going online and load the file you just saved.

The **\<DL\>** tag for starting the **DEFINITION** list function precedes the **\<DT\>** title tag.

\<DL\>

\<DT\>Fruit:

\<DD\>Apples

\<DD\>Oranges

\<DD\>Bananas

\<DD\>Pears

\</DL\>

110

Fruit:

<UL>

<LI>Apples

<LI>Oranges

<LI>Bananas

<LI>Pears

</UL>

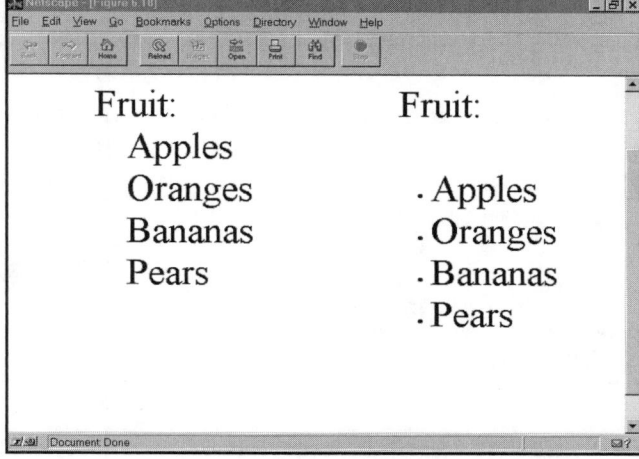

The Web page produced by our list examples (the text magnified using <FONT SIZE=7>). Note that the <UL> tag inserted a line break, and that the bullets did not get larger when the text got larger.

Creating Enhanced Lists

You'll notice that the **UNORDERED**, **MENU**, and **DIRECTORY** lists all sport bullets. Webmasters have longed to control those bullets, and the Web-powers-that-be have responded with the **TYPE** element, as detailed in the following table. **TYPE** lets you set the bullet to be a circle, square, or disc (a solid circle, the default value).

Table 6.8 *UNORDERED* Bullet Elements

Type	Syntax of Beginning Tag
Circle	**<UL TYPE=CIRCLE>**
Square	**<UL TYPE=SQUARE>**
Disc	**<UL TYPE=DISC>**

However, simple numbers proved insufficient for an **ORDERED** list. Therefore, we now have ways to order the list in a customized fashion, as shown in the following table. Also detailed is the **START** element, which lets you start the list's numbering scheme at something other than one.

Table 6.9 *ORDERED* List Numbering Options

Syntax	Numbering Method
<OL TYPE=A>	Uppercase letters instead of numbers
<OL TYPE=a>	Lowercase letters instead of numbers
<OL TYPE=I>	Uppercase Roman numerals instead of numbers
<OL TYPE=i>	Lowercase Roman numerals instead of numbers
<OL TYPE=1>	Numbers (default)
<OL TYPE=A START=7>	Start numbering at 7 (G, if using **TYPE=A**)

You can put lists within lists (called nesting), and the ability to use different numbering methods with **TYPE** makes it a powerful tool for organizing material.

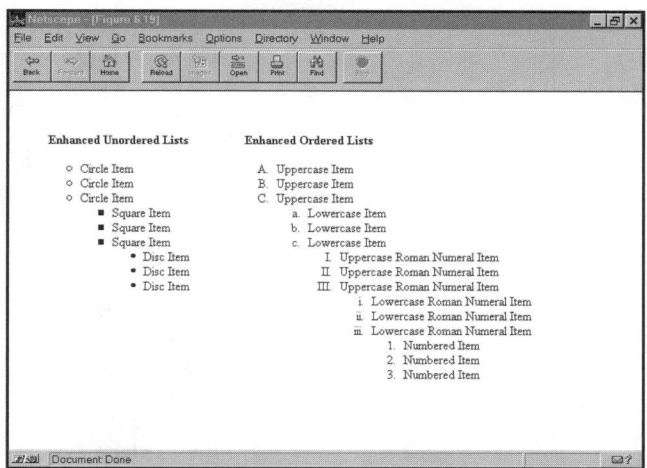

The effect of using enhanced lists. Using a scheme of different bullets and numbering schemes, you can create a sort of outline hierarchy.

To use an enhanced **ORDERED** or **UNORDERED** list format in an HTML file, do the following.

Fruit:

<UL>

<LI>Apples

<LI>Oranges

<LI>Bananas

<LI>Pears

</UL>

1 **Create an** ORDERED **or** UNORDERED **list as described in the previous section.**

2 **If it is an** UNORDERED **list, decide what bullet you want to use. Inside the** <UL> **tag, add** TYPE= CIRCLE, TYPE=SQUARE, **or** TYPE=DISC, **and then skip to Step 5.**

113

Fruit:

\<OL\>

\<LI\>Apples

\<LI\>Orange

\<LI\>Bananas

\<LI\>Pears

\</OL\>

Fruit:

\<UL TYPE=SQUARE\>

\<LI\>Apples

\<LI\>Oranges

\<LI\>Bananas

\<LI\>Pears

\</UL\>

3 If it is an ORDERED list, decide what kind of numbering you want: numbers, upper- or lowercase letters, or upper- or lowercase Roman numerals. Inside the \<OL\> tag, insert either TYPE=A, TYPE=a, TYPE=I, TYPE=i, or TYPE=1.

4 If it is an ORDERED list, determine if you need to begin at a number other than one. If so, after the TYPE= element, add START=X, where X is the number you want to start with.

5 Save the file, making sure it remains in the ASCII text-only format and retains the .htm extension. In some word processors, you may have to close the file as well.

6 Now test the file. Launch your browser without going online and load the file you just saved.

Fruit:

<OL TYPE=A>

<LI>Apples

<LI>Oranges

<LI>Bananas

<LI>Pears

</OL>

Fruit:

<OL TYPE=I START=7>

<LI>Apples

<LI>Oranges

<LI>Bananas

<LI>Pears

</OL>

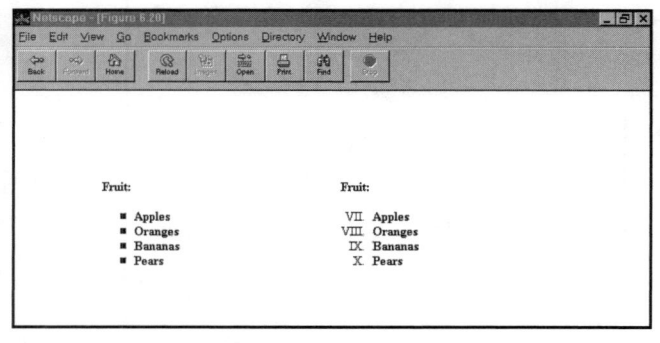

The Web page produced by our two examples, using square bullets, and Roman numerals starting at VII.

115

Using Text and Graphics as Links

Besides the ability to format graphics and text together on a page, the second major attraction of the Web is hypertext: the ability to link items together so that clicking one item will call up the other item to which it is linked. Hypertext links can also trigger other actions, such as sending e-mail, or downloading files.

Hypertext can be thought of as automated footnotes. With a footnote, you see that the text has a citation marker, so you glance to the bottom of the page, the end of the chapter, or the back of the book to see the note the author is referencing. Then, you go back to the spot where you were interrupted and begin reading again.

Similarly, with Web hypertext on graphical browsers, the user sees that an item (an image, word, sentence…whatever) is linked. This linkage is indicated with some kind of highlighting, usually an underscore and distinct coloration. (Sometimes, the only visual hint that there's a hyperlink is the cursor changing to a pointing hand.) Our example shows the corporate Web page before and after links were added.

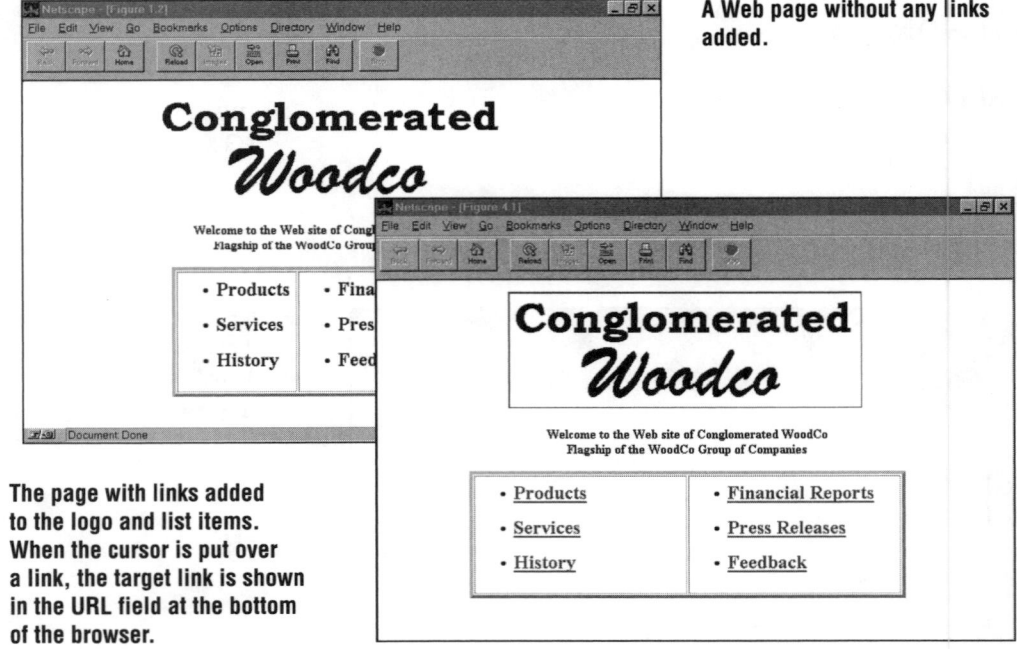

A Web page without any links added.

The page with links added to the logo and list items. When the cursor is put over a link, the target link is shown in the URL field at the bottom of the browser.

116

With most browsers, the user can redefine the style in which links are displayed. And, as we'll see in Part IX, you can set the colors to be used for links on a Web page.

The user can then click the link and be taken to whatever material is being linked. That material can be another file on that site, another file on a server on the other side of the globe, or another paragraph farther down the page. Having satisfied himself or herself, the user can then return to the original page by using the browser's BACK screen button. (The page's designer may also have added navigation buttons on the page to bring the user back.)

The concept of automated footnotes only scratches the surface of what can be done with hypertext links. Pages can be linked to multiple pages, and then back to one another, and then to other sites. The reader can find answers to almost any question that pops into his or her head. Every avenue of inquiry can be explored. Furthermore, your site can be linked to outside sites, if only through search engine references. Indeed, the contents of the Web can be thought of as a single, huge set of interlinked documents—a *World Wide Web*.

The way hyperlinks are added to Web files is through **anchor tags**.

As covered in Part V, images are added to a Web file by using the **IMG** function of HTML. As you might imagine, the line of HTML code of our example page that displays the logo (a file called logo.gif) would look like this:

\<IMG SRC="logo.gif"\>

To link this image to a file called bgrnd.html (a page containing, presumably, corporate background information), we would precede the **IMG** tag with an anchor tag, and follow it with an end tag.

The anchor tag looks like this:

\<A HREF="bgrnd.html"\>

The **\<A\>** ("Anchor") tag is the hypertext link. The **HREF** (HTTP Reference) element states the name of the file to which you will link (which must be in quotation marks). The **IMG** tag is then inserted, and is followed by the anchor end tag, **\</A\>**.

Altogether, our linked image looks like this in HTML:

\<A HREF="bgrnd.html"\>\<IMG SRC="logo.gif"\>\</A\>

Everything between the **\<A\>** and **\</A\>** tags will be marked as a link. In this case, it's just one image, and the result is an image surrounded by a box, as in our example.

117

When using the **<A>** anchor element, don't forget to put in the **</A>** end tag. Otherwise, the rest of the page starting from the anchor tag will become one huge link—which is probably not what you want.

It is also possible that the file you are linking to is in another subdirectory on the server, or on another Web site entirely. In that case, simply using the file name will not do, and you will have to include a file path, or an entire URL. See Table 7.1, which shows addressing modes.

Table 7.1   Addressing Modes

Mode	Syntax
Local	thefile.htm
Local, deeper directory	/morefiles/thefile.htm
Local, higher directory	../../webstuff/file.
Remote URL	http://www.there.com/thefile.htm

Now let's look at another operative line of code from our examples, the code used to link to one of the list items:

<A HREF="prods.html">Products</A>

Next, we will link text instead of an image: the word Products from the list of links on the page. It is preceded by the **<A>** tag, with the **HREF** element referencing a file named prods.html. The result is that Products is colored and underlined on the page, showing that it is linked. If Products is clicked, the browser calls up the file named prods.html. Again, everything between the **<A>** and the **</A>** tags is part of the link.

There are actually three different ways to use HTML hyperlinks:

- *Remote*: Jumps to another file, anywhere on the Internet.

- *Remote, named*: Jumps to a point in another file. The point must have been previously assigned a name using the **<A NAME=>** anchor tag. (Although it is not used often, this option is quite useful.)

- *Local*: Jumps to a point in the same file that you are already in. The point must have been previously assigned a name using the **<A NAME=>** anchor tag.

The jumps are handled by the **HREF** element of the anchor tag. Table 7.2 provides the details. In the next sections, we'll look at how to use each method and how to add a **NAME** tag.

Table 7.2   Anchor Tag Elements

Element	Syntax	Comment
HREF (remote)	`<A HREF="X">~</A>`	Jumps to a file with the name X when the tagged material is clicked.
HREF (local)	`<A HREF="#name">~</A>`	Jumps to a named point in the file that you are already in when the tagged material is clicked.
HREF (remote, named)	`<A HREF "X#Y">~</A>`	Jumps to a point in file X that has been given the name Y when the tagged material is clicked.
NAME	`<A NAME="X">~</A>`	Assigns a name to the tagged material so that the local or remote-named HREF tag can jump to it.
TARGET	`<A HREF="X" TARGET="Y">~</A>`	Opens the linked file X in a window bearing the name Y. This is a Netscape enhancement and is used with frames, as discussed in Part XII.

Using the **NAME** element, you can jump to a precise point in a file. Without it, you can only jump to the top of a new file. And if the **NAME** element in the link cannot be found, you will simply jump to the top of the new file.

Adding a Remote Link

To add a link to a remote file, proceed as follows:

1 Determine the name of the file you want to link to from the page you are working on. If it is in the same subdirectory, you only need the name. If it is in a different subdirectory on the same server, you need the file path as well. If it is in another server on the Web, you need the full URL.

2 We'll assume it is in the same subdirectory and is named here.htm.

3 Open the HTML file you want to put the link in, using Notepad or a word processor that can use the ASCII format.

4 Find the element in the file that you want to be the hypertext link. It can be an image or text.

5 Directly in front of the item, add the anchor tag with the HREF element.

6 Directly after the linked element, add the </A> end tag.

7 Save the file in ASCII text-only format by using the .htm extension. In some word processors, you may have to close the file as well.

8 Now test the file. Launch your browser without going online and load the file by using the load local file command. Make sure the hyperlinks are where you want them. Click them to see whether they actually work. (If they are present in the same subdirectory, they should. If you linked to a file on a remote server, the link should work if you go online.)

```
<IMG SRC="filename.gif>          ⎤
                                  ⎬ 4
<H5>Click Here</H5>              ⎦

<A HREF="here.htm"><H5>Click Here</H5>             ⎤
                                                   ⎬ 5
<A HREF="here.htm"><IMG SRC="filename.gif>        ⎦

<A HREF="here.htm"><H5>Click Here</H5></A>             ⎤
                                                       ⎬ 6
<A HREF="here.htm"><IMG SRC="filename.gif></A>        ⎦
```

At the start of your project, contact your Web server administrator to determine the file-naming conventions you need to follow (including case-sensitivity), based on the platform the server is running on. If in doubt, use lowercase characters and the .HTM extension. See Part XIV for more details.

Adding a Local Link

A local link is a hyperlink that will take you to a different point in the same file that you are already in—presumably somewhere below the bottom of the initial visible area. The point being jumped to must be marked with a **NAME** element, which will be discussed later.

To add a local link, proceed as follows:

```
<A NAME="here">logo.gif</A>

<A NAME="here">Chapter Two</A>
```
⎤ 2

```
<IMG SRC="logo.gif>

Click Here
```
⎤ 3

```
<A HREF="#here"><IMG SRC="logo.gif>

<A HREF="#here"><Click Here
```
⎤ 4

```
<A HREF="#here"><IMG SRC="logo.gif></A>

<A HREF="#here">Click Here</A>
```
⎤ 5

1 Open the HTML file you want to add the link to, using Notepad, or a word processor that can use the ASCII format.

2 Find the NAME element in the file that you want to jump to with the link. As shown in the following, it can be an image tag or any text.

3 Find the element in the file that you want to be the hypertext link—i.e., the place you want to jump from. It could be an image tag, or any text, as shown here.

4 Directly in front of the item, add the anchor tag with the NAME element preceded by the # sign, in quotation marks.

5 Then add the </A> end tag.

6 Save the file in ASCII format using the .htm extension. In some word processors, you may have to close the file as well.

7 Now test the file. Launch your browser without going online and load the file using the load local file command. Make sure the hyperlinks are where you want them. Click them to see if they actually work.

Adding the *NAME* Element

Local file links and named remote file links have one thing in common: They both require that the file being linked to have a **NAME** element. The **NAME** element provides the "target" that the hyperlink can jump to. If you do not use the **NAME** element, or use it incorrectly, the link will jump to the top of the new file.

To add a **NAME** element to a file so that it can be jumped to, from the outside or from another spot in the same file, proceed as follows:

1 Open the file to which you want to add the NAME element, using Notepad or a word processor that can use the ASCII format.

2 Determine a point in the file that you think it would convenient to jump to, either from the inside or the outside. Presumably, a good place for this would be either a section header, or an important image.

```
<H2>Chapter Two</H2> ⎤
                     ⎬ 2
<IMG SCR=usamap.gif> ⎦
```

```
<A NAME="here"><H2>Chapter Two</H2>        ⎤
                                           ⎬ 4
<A NAME="here"><IMG SCR=usamap.gif>        ⎦
```

```
<A NAME="here"><H2>Chapter Two</H2></A>    ⎤
                                           ⎬ 5
<A NAME="here"><IMG SCR=usamap.gif></A>    ⎦
```

When viewed via a browser, there is no indication of the presence of a **NAME** element in a file.

3 Decide on a name for that point. We'll use "here."

4 In front of the item to carry the name, add the anchor tag. Note that the name is in quotation marks.

5 Following the item that is to carry the name, add the end tag.

6 Save the file in ASCII format using the .htm extension. In some word processors, you may have to close the file as well.

7 Now test the file. Launch your browser without going online and load the file using the load local file command. Try linking to the file from another file that has an anchor tag with a named remote link to that file. If you end up at the top of the file instead of at the NAME element, the link did not function correctly.

Adding a Remote, Named Link

With a named link to a remote file, you can click the hyperlink in the local file and jump to a specific spot in the remote file. The remote file has to have a **NAME** element in it, and you have to use that name as part of the anchor tag. (Without the name, or with a wrong name, you jump to the top of the remote file.)

To add a named link to the remote file, proceed as follows:

1 Examine the file to which you want to jump to find a NAME element to use. If it is one of your own files, simply open it with a word processor. If it is someone else's file on a remote server, you can examine it using your browser's View Source command.

2 The NAME element can be attached to an image file or a string of text, as shown here.

3 Make note of the file's name. If it is to be in another subdirectory, note its file path. If it is on another server, get its full URL.

4 Open the file from which you want to jump (i.e., add the link to) using Notepad or a word processor that can use the ASCII format.

```
<A NAME="here"><IMG SCR=filename.gif></A>    ⎤
                                             ⎬ 2
<A NAME="here">Chapter Two</A>               ⎦
```

5 Find the element in that file that you want to be the hypertext link—i.e., the place from which you want to jump. It could be an image file or text, as follows.

```
<IMG SRC="logo.gif">    ⎤
                        ⎬ 5
Click Here              ⎦
```

6 Directly in front of the item, add the anchor tag with the HREF= element. Then add the file's name, with the path or full URL if need be. Then add the NAME that you located in the remote file, preceded by the # sign. The whole entry should be in quotation marks.

```
<A HREF="here.htm#here"><IMG SRC="logo.gif">    ⎤
                                                ⎬ 6
<A HREF="here.htm#here">Click Here              ⎦
```

To see if a Web page has a **NAME** element that you can link to, you will need to view its raw HTML code. To do that in Netscape Navigator, select View, Document Source. In Microsoft Internet Explorer, select View, Source.

```
<A HREF="here.htm#here"><IMG SRC="logo.gif"></A>
```
7

```
<A HREF="here.htm#here">Click Here</A>
```
9

7 Directly after the linked element, add the </A> end tag.

8 Save the file in ASCII format by using the .htm extension. In some word processors, you may have to close the file as well.

9 Now test the file. Launch your browser without going online and load the file using the load local file command. Click the hyperlinks to see if they actually work. If both are in the same subdirectory, or if the link uses a functional path name, the links should work when tested inside your PC. If one file is at a remote URL, the link should work if you go online.

While viewing a Web page on your browser, you can save it to your computer by using the browser's File Save command. Later, you can examine the HTML code using a word processor.

Removing Borders from Linked Images

An image used as a link has a border around it, using whatever color the Web page (or the browser, if no colors are specified) is using to designate linked elements, as in this example.

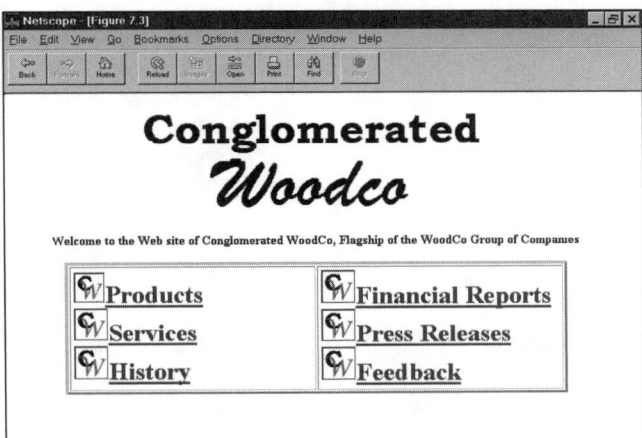

Both the icons and the title words in the box are linked and therefore carry highlights—which means there is a border around each icon.

You might regard this colored border as a good thing. But, if you are striving for balanced color composition, you might be deeply aggrieved. Fortunately, the outline can be erased using the **BORDER** attribute of the **IMG** tag. (The user will still know it's a link because the cursor will turn into a pointing hand when it passes over the item.)

To remove an outline you find offensive, proceed as follows:

1 Open the file that contains the image with the outline by using Notepad or a word processor that uses the ASCII format.

2 Locate the IMG tag of the image with the outline. If the image is named icon.gif, then the tag would look something like this.

125

```
<A HREF="here.htm"><IMG BORDER=0
➥SRC="icon.gif"></A>
```
⌐3

3 Inside the IMG tag, insert BORDER=0.

4 Save the file by using the .htm extension, in the ASCII format. In some word processors, you may have to close it as well.

5 Now test the file. Launch your browser without going online and load the file you just saved by using its load local file command. Hopefully, the outline will have disappeared, as in the next example.

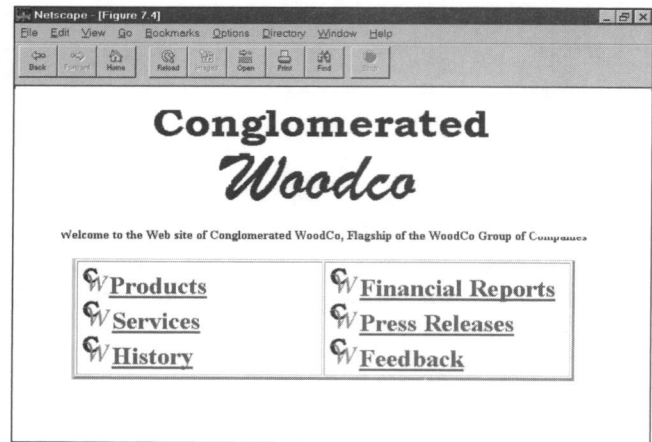

The borders are now gone from the icons, although they are still linked. The text is not affected. The cursor will still turn into a pointing hand when it passes over one of the icons.

Multiple Links per Image

Instead of just clicking an image to jump to a preset location, it is possible to have multiple links assigned to different parts of an image. Parts of the area can be mapped to a particular link, and clicking that part of the image will trigger the jump.

You can find out more about Live Image and how to download it in Part XV, "Web Graphics Tools and Sources."

Such features are called *image maps*. In fact, they don't need to be maps, but maps are the most obvious application. For instance, a page on a corporate site might show a world map. Clicking a continent would trigger a jump to a page containing sales contact information concerning the countries on that continent.

Adding an image map to a Web page requires (of course) an image you intend to use as a map. Beyond that, a set of X-Y pixel coordinates must be created that divides up the image into clickable areas. And the link for each area must be stored. This data, correctly formatted, must be added to the HTML file. Then, the **IMG** tag of the image being used as the map must be linked to that data.

Fortunately, there is software that executes these chores automatically. We will assume the use of one such program, called Live Image. Information on acquiring it is in Part XV.

What we are doing is client-side mapping. That means that the map data is integrated into the HTML file, and the browser interprets the mouse click and decides what link to invoke. With older server-side maps, the map coordinates had to be loaded into a separate file on the server, the HTML files had to invoke a utility on the server, and the server interpreted the mouse clicks. Such image maps could not be tested offline, and the latest generation of browsers makes them unnecessary.

Mapping Images

Using Live Image or similar software, you can turn an image contained in an existing Web page into an image map. You can map out the clickable areas that you want to add to the image, and assign links. The software will add the necessary code to the page's HTML file.

To create an image map with Live Image, proceed as follows:

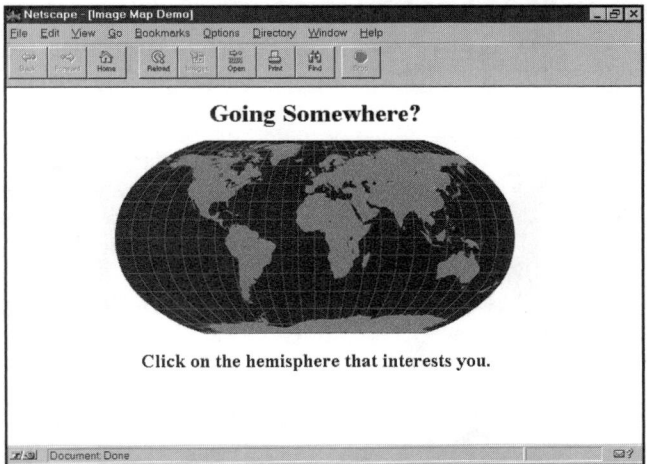

1 Create a Web page with the image in question, as detailed throughout this book, especially Part V.

2 Call up Live Image. In the opening screen, select the New Image Map Wizard.

3 Click OK. The Create A New Image Map window appears.

4 Select the existing HTML file option.

5 Click Next. The file selection window appears.

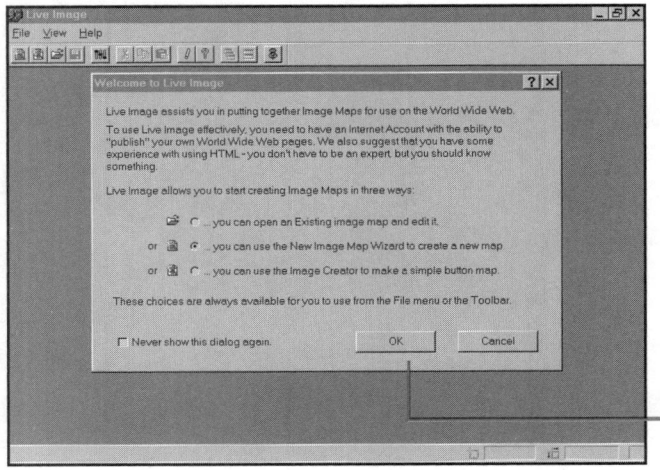

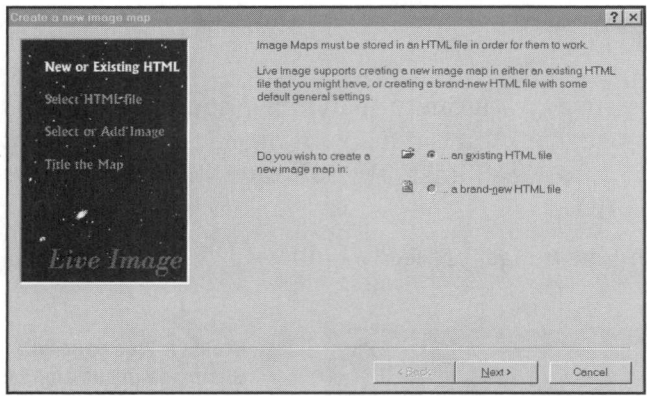

6 Navigate through the file structure and click the HTML file that you want to add an image map to. Live Image will tell you how many maps and images are in the file.

7 Click Next. The image selection window appears.

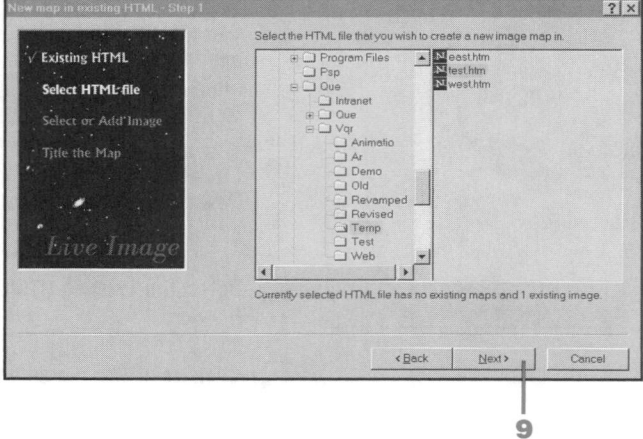

9

8 From the list, select the image that you want to use as the image map. (In this case, there is only one.) After clicking it, a thumbnail version of the image will appear in the preview window.

9 Click Next. The name selection window appears.

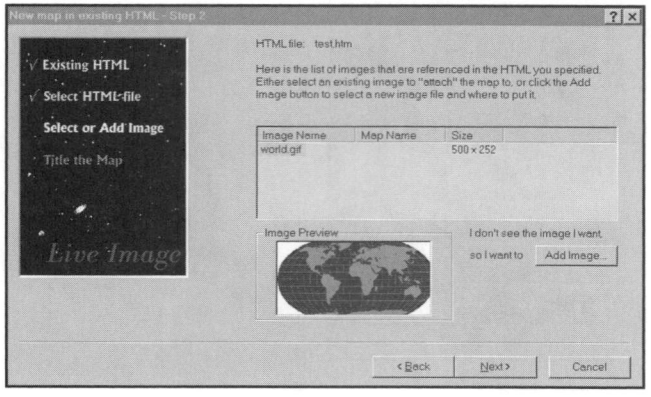

10 The software needs a name to assign to the image map for its internal use. Depending on the complexity of the HTML file, this may be a trivial matter or a troublesome one. Input a name that will not be troublesome. The name of the file is selected by default, which in this case is fine.

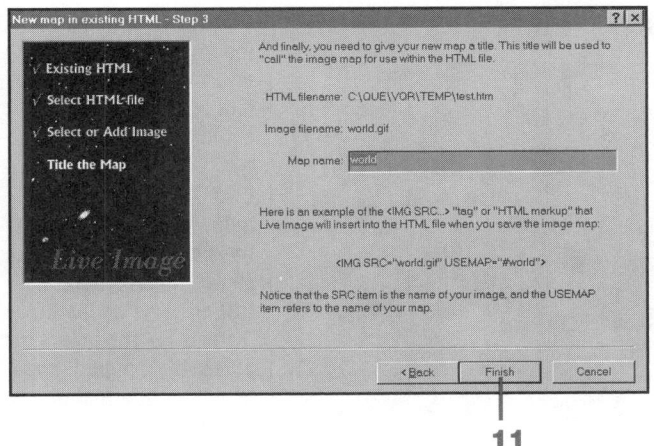

11

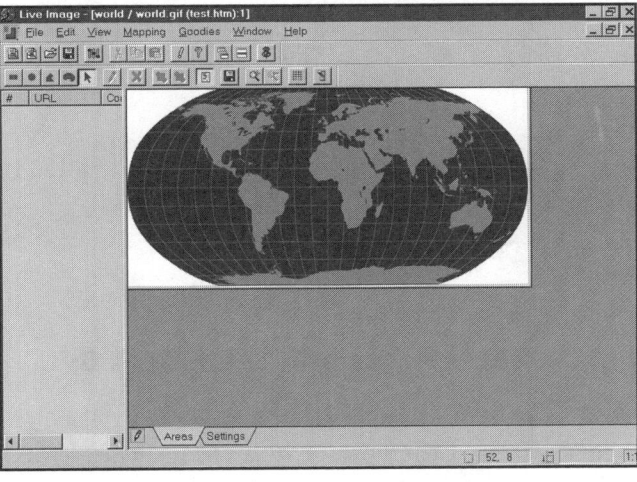

11 Click Finish. The image mapping screen appears.

12 You can map out clickable areas with a rectangle, circle, and polygon tool. We'll assume the use of the rectangle tool. Click it.

13 The rectangle tool appears. Click in one corner of the area you want to map, and click-drag it to the other corner. The mapped area will be shaded, as shown.

14 The Area Setting window appears. Input the file that this area is linked to.

15 Click OK.

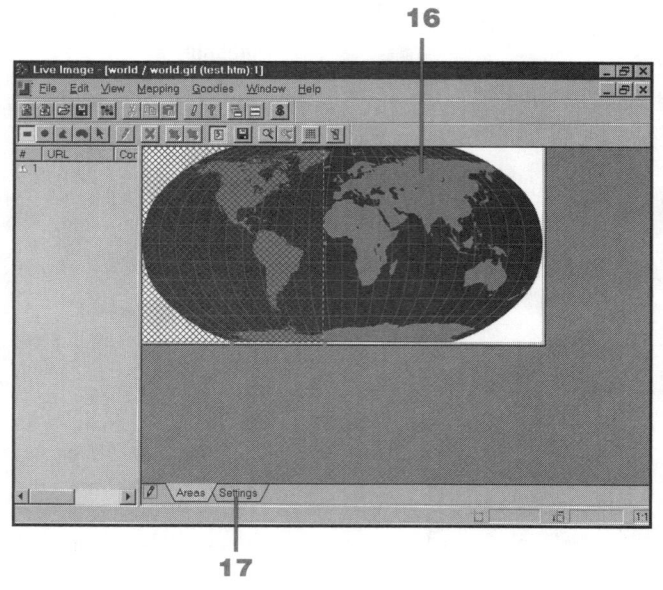

16

17

16 Proceed to map the rest of the image, shading the areas with the appropriate tool and then filling in the settings.

17 Click the Settings tab below the image. The settings window appears, as shown. Input a default URL to serve as the link for areas of the image not otherwise mapped, and any other information you care to enter.

18 Save the file using the File, Save commands.

The HTML file is saved, with modifications. For instance, the **IMG** tag, which controls the placement and appearance of the image on the page (as detailed in Part V), may have looked like this:

<IMG SRC="world.gif">

It now looks like this:

<IMG SRC="world.gif" USEMAP="#world" BORDER=0>

As detailed in Part V, the **BORDER=0** element means that a heavy border will not be placed around the image, as would otherwise be done to indicate a link. You can change this if desired by editing the file, as detailed in Part V.

The **USEMAP** element indicates that this image is mapped, and the name that follows indicates which MAP tag (there can be more than one) in the HTML file contains the coordinates of the image map.

Near the bottom of the file, a **MAP** tag has been inserted, followed by **AREA** tags giving the X-Y pixel coordinates of the borders of each area you mapped in the image, using Live Image.

Our example, with its image converted into an image map, appears as shown. The only outward difference is that the cursor will turn into a hand as it crosses a mapped area, and the destination URL appears in the lower-left corner.

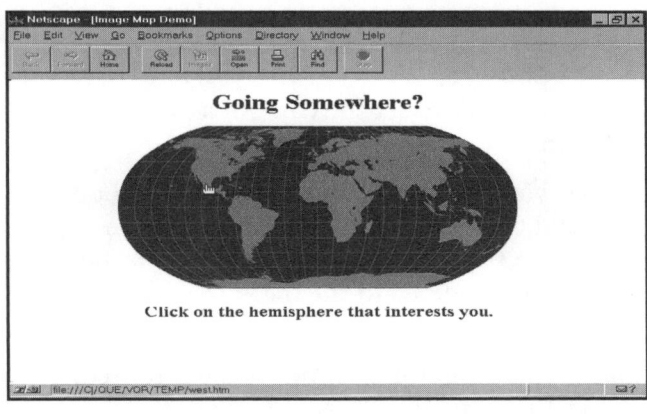

Web page with link cursor.

133

Adding Backgrounds to Web Pages

It is possible, using simple HTML functions, to set the color of a Web page's background and the color of its text.

However, doing so will require that you use RGB color values. The RGB method breaks a shade into its Red, Blue, and Green components. Each separate component is assigned a value, depending on the intensity of its presence in the shade, from 0 to 255. Next, these numbers are rendered in the (base-16) "hexadecimal" number system.

Then, having decided or estimated what the two-digit hex value is for red, green, and blue, you run them together into one six-digit hex number.

For instance, assume you want to use the color blue. Red and green are not employed and, therefore, are each **00**, but blue is at its full value of 255, or **FF** in hexadecimal. So the resulting RGB value would be: **0000FF**.

Online renderings of RGB colors can be viewed at **http://colors.infi.net/ colorindex2.html**.

You can generate a hex RGB value for any color in an image using Paint Shop Pro and the Windows Calculator. You can find Calculator in the Accessories item in the Startup menu of Windows 95.

1. Call up the Calculator, and use the View, Scientific commands.

2. In Paint Shop Pro, click the eyedropper tool and place the eyedropper icon on a pixel in the image containing the color you want to use. The value for red, blue, and green is shown as you do so, just below the color-in-use indicator on the right. However, these are decimal values.

3. Switch over to the Calculator and click the Dec (decimal) radio button.

4. Input the value for red.

5. Click the Hex (hexadecimal) radio button. The value you just entered will be converted into the hexadecimal value you need for red.

6. Repeat the procedure for green and blue, making sure the Dec radio button is clicked when you input the number, and then click the Hex button.

7. Combine the three hex values into the RGB value you need.

Obviously, the number of colors that can be defined this way is enormous. If there's an official corporate color scheme you want to emulate, you can probably do so, although some experimentation might be necessary. Table 9.1 indicates starting points for your color searches.

Table 9.1 RGB Color Examples

Color	RRGGBB Value	Color	RRGGBB Value
Black	000000	Purple	FF00FF
White	FFFFFF	Yellow	FFFF00
Red	FF0000	Brown	996633
Green	00FF00	Orange	FF8000
Azure	00FFFF	Violet	8000FF
Blue	0000FF	Gray	A0A0A0

The trend among browsers has been to support colors by name. However, there is little agreement between browsers: Netscape Navigator supports 138 predefined color names. Microsoft Internet Explorer supports only 16. The following lists show the color names (which should be written as one word even when they are obviously two or three words):

Microsoft Internet Explorer:

Aqua	**Green**	**Olive**	**Teal**
Black	**Lime**	**Purple**	**White**
Blue	**Maroon**	**Red**	**Yellow**
Fuchsia	**Gray**	**Navy**	**Silver**

Netscape Navigator:

Aliceblue	Darkmagenta	Hotpink
Antiquewhite	Darkolivegreen	Indianred
Aqua	Darkorange	Indigo
Aquamarine	Darkorchid	Ivory
Azure	Darkred	Khaki
Beige	Darksalmon	Lavender
Bisque	Darkseagreen	Lavenderblush
Black	Darkslateblue	Lawngreen
Blanchedalmond	Darkslategray	Lemonchiffon
Blue	Darkturquoise	Lightblue
Blueviolet	Darkviolet	Lightcoral
Brown	Deeppink	Lightcyan
Burlywood	Deepskyblue	Lightgoldenrodyellow
Cadetblue	Dimgray	Lightgreen
Chartreuse	Dodgerblue	Lightgray
Chocolate	Firebrick	Lightpink
Coral	Floralwhite	Lightsalmon
Cornflowerblue	Forestgreen	Lightseagreen
Cornsilk	Fuchsia	Lightskyblue
Crimson	Gainsboro	Lightslategray
Cyan	Ghostwhite	Lightyellow
Darkblue	Gold	Lime
Darkcyan	Goldenrod	Limegreen
Darkgoldenrod	Gray	Linen
Darkgray	Green	Magenta
Darkgreen	Greenyellow	Maroon
Darkhaki	Honeydew	Mediumaquamarine

Mediumblue	Orchid	Sienna
Mediumorchid	Palegoldenrod	Silver
Mediumpurple	Palegreen	Skyblue
Mediumseagreen	Paleturquoise	Slateblue
Mediumslateblue	Palevioletred	Snow
Mediumspringgreen	Peachpuff	Springgreen
Mediumturquoise	Peru	Steelblue
Mediumvioletred	Pink	Tan
Midnightblue	Plum	Teal
Mintcream	Powderblue	Thistle
Mistyrose	Purple	Tomato
Moccasin	Red	Turquoise
Navajowhite	Rosybrown	Violet
Navy	Royalblue	Wheat
Oldlace	Saddlebrown	White
Olive	Salmon	Whitesmoke
Olivedrab	Sandybrown	Yellow
Orange	Seagreen	Yellowgreen
Orangered	Seashell	

Shareware software that will help you define color by RGB values is available for downloading. These include Color Manipulation Device from Quality Software, and Colorwiz from Game Tool Technologies. Acquiring them is covered in Part XV.

Changing Background Colors

You can change the background color of a Web page by adding the **BGCOLOR** element to the **<BODY>** tag.

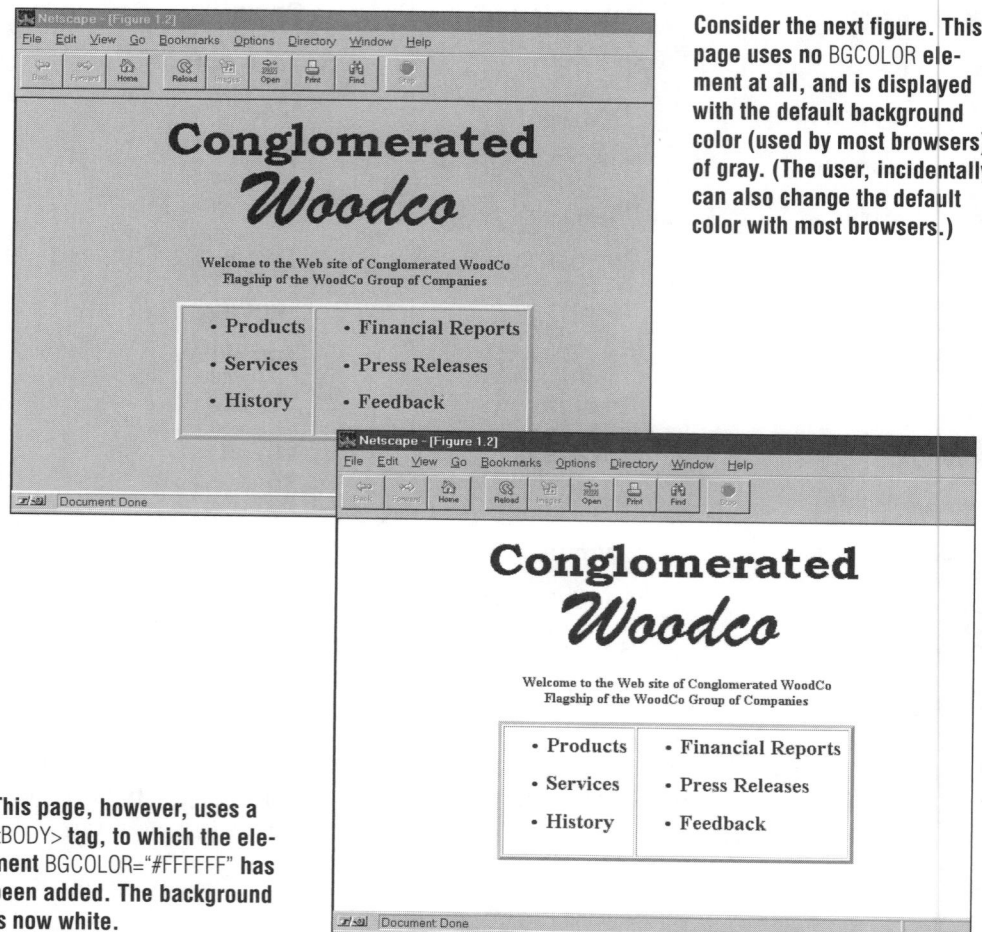

Consider the next figure. This page uses no BGCOLOR element at all, and is displayed with the default background color (used by most browsers) of gray. (The user, incidentally, can also change the default color with most browsers.)

This page, however, uses a <BODY> tag, to which the element BGCOLOR="#FFFFFF" has been added. The background is now white.

You can change the background color to any shade that can be represented by the RGB format. For that matter, there is no human agency that can stop you from having a black background behind black letters.

(If RGB is not enough, you can also resort to using a solid-color image as the page background, using the method described in Adding Background Images later in this chapter. This will have the effect of setting the background color. But it will also mean that the user will have another file to download.)

Browsers increasingly support named colors, so that you don't have to use RGB values. Our example could be **BGCOLOR="white"**. However, for broader compatibility, sticking with Hexadecimal RGB is probably wiser.

To add a background color to your Web page, proceed as follows:

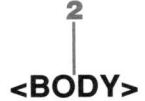

<BODY>

<BODY BGCOLOR="#FFFFFF>"

3

1 Determine the RGB value or the browser-supported name of the color you want to use.

2 Locate the <BODY> tag in the HTML file whose background color you wish to change. It should be in the first lines of the file.

3 Insert the BGCOLOR= element into the tag, followed by the RGB value or the name. The value or name should begin with the # sign and be enclosed in quotes.

4 Save the file using the ASCII text-only format. In some word processors, you may also have to close it.

5 Test the file. Bring up your browser offline and view the file using the load local file command.

Setting Default Text Colors

In addition to changing the background color of the page, you can also change the default colors of the text. There are actually four different modes of text that the browsers identify, and you can distinguish them with different colors. (Or, if having all these colors on the page offends you, make them all the same color.) The following table lays them out.

Table 9.2   Color Text Modes

Mode	Syntax	Comment
Normal	TEXT="#000000"	This is the default color for all text on the page that is not included in one of the follwing modes.
Hyperlinks	LINK="#008200"	This is the color in which linked text will be displayed, as well as being underlined.
Visited Links	VLINK="#551A8B"	Links to which the user has already visited and returned from will be shown in this color. The visit could be in the same session or in the previous month, depending on the browser settings.
Active Links	ALINK="#EE0000"	Linked text will turn this color after the user clicks it and before the new page appears. Depending on the user's connection speed, this could be a moment, or an extended period. (This element is not used much anymore.)

Changing text color using the **<FONT COLOR>** tag, discussed in Part VI, overrides text colors set by the **<BODY>** tag. However, **<BODY>** text color settings override browser text color settings—except the colors of links.

To set the default text colors on a page, proceed as follows.

2

<BODY>

<BODY TEXT="#FFFFFF"
LINK="#A0A0A0" VLINK="#808080"

3

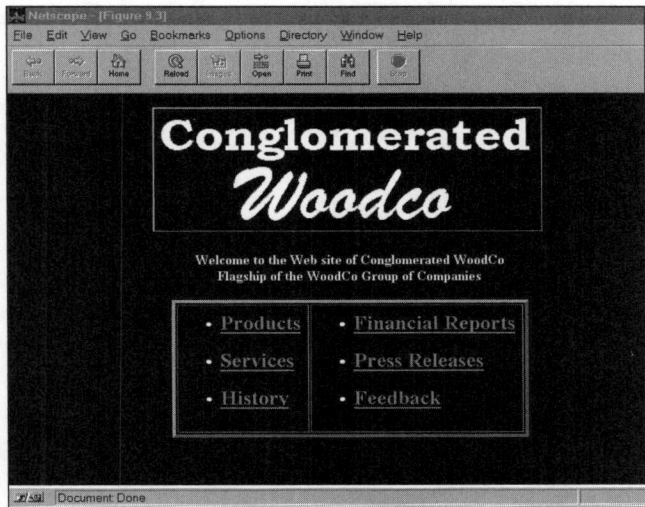

ALINK="#808080" >

1 Determine the color scheme you want in terms of RGB values, picking colors from the previous RGB list, or by determining the RGB value of colors you are interested in using Paint Shop Pro and the Windows Calculator, as described in the beginning of this chapter.

2 Locate the <BODY> tag of the Web page's HTML file.

3 Insert the TEXT, LINK, VLINK, and, if desired, ALINK elements, with their respective RGB values. The values should be preceded by the # sign and enclosed in quotes, as shown.

4 Save the file in the ASCII text-only format. In some word processors, you may have to close it as well.

5 Test it by loading it into your browser, offline, using the load-file command.

Adding Background Images

Using the **BACKGROUND** element of the **\<BODY>** tag, you can use an image as the background for the page, creating a sort of "watermark stationery" or "wallpaper" or "texture" for the page. The image need not be the same size as the page, as the browser will *tile* it across the page, as the next two figures show. (Keep in mind that the wallpaper images download as slowly as other images, so keep them small.)

The Web page with background image—a large, pale version of the corporate logo—added as a "watermark."

There are several considerations:

- The borders of the image need to appear so that the image looks natural when tiled. (You can get around the tiling issue by using an image with large dimensions—the image will tile, but the viewer will not ordinarily stretch the browser window into a size that requires the image to tile.)

- The colors, patterns, and textures of the background image must not obscure the overlying text.

- Whatever background color (**BGCOLOR** element) is used will be the color of any image borders and table borders, and will "show through" the background image.

- Likewise, if you use a transparent color in the background image, the background color can show through the image.

142

■ The background image will appear to be part of the background for any other images on the page that use transparent color backgrounds, as in our previous Web page example.

To add a background image to a Web page, proceed as follows.

\<BODY\>

\<BODY BACKGROUND="texture.gif"\>

3

1 Determine what file you want to use for the background.

2 Locate the \<BODY\> tag in the HTML file of the Web page in which you want to put the background image.

3 Add the BACKGROUND element, as shown, with the file name in quotation marks.

4 Save the file in the ASCII text-only format. In some word processors, you may also have to close it.

5 Test the file by loading it into your browser while offline, using the load local file command.

As in all cases where you add references to file names, remember that most Web servers are "case-sensitive," so that texture.gif and TEXTURE.GIF will be seen as different file names.

For maximum compatibility, the background image should be in the GIF or JPG format.

Animated GIFs

A little-known fact (that is, little-known until the Web became a force to take seriously) is that the GIF format includes a facility for encoding more than one image. Using software that can support this feature, images can be displayed in succession in the same frame. And that's really all that cartoons and movies are: images shown in succession. The only thing lacking is sound.

And the latest generation of browsers does support multi-image GIF files. After being created, they can be added to an HTML file exactly like any other GIF. When the browser displays them on the page, the animation runs automatically, running once or looping endlessly, as desired. **No further programming is necessary.**

Before proceeding, you need to understand that GIF files arrange their data in "blocks." Each block has a separate function, and each image has a separate set of blocks, described as follows:

- **Header Block.** Contains the size of the file, the background color, the number of colors in use, and whether the color palette is global (shared by other images in the file) or local to that image. (For Web animations, use global palettes.)

- **Image Block.** Contains the image itself, interlacing information, and any local palette used by the image. It can also specify the size of the image (inside the frame created by the header block) and any offset inside that frame.

- **Control Block.** Contains color transparency information, timing information (for the speed the animation will run), and a facility for tying the start of the animation to user input. (This last feature is not currently supported by browsers.)

- **Comment Block.** For text that will appear only with certain GIF editors.

- **Loop Block.** If present, the animation will loop continually. (It includes an optional iteration counter to stop the looping eventually, but it is not widely supported.)

- **Application Block.** For specialized purposes.

A GIF file must contain at least the header and image blocks. For GIF animations, there is usually a progression of blocks:

1. Header Block

2. Loop Block

3. Control Block for the first image

4. Image Block for the first image

5. Control Block for the second image

6. Image Block for the second image

7. And so on, with any further Control and Image Blocks

8. Optional Comment Block

The software steps through the GIF file, displaying each Image Block in turn according to the instructions of the preceding Control Block. If there is a Loop Block, it starts over after the end.

For the purposes of creating an animation, there are three main considerations:

■ You must have software that can edit and assemble the blocks inside a GIF file. We will assume the use of the GIF Construction Set, a shareware program available for downloading from Alchemy Mindworks, Inc. Acquisition information is in Part XV.

■ You must have a set of images in the GIF format that, if displayed in succession, will produce the effect of animation. As we will discuss later, it is possible to produce them from AVI video files. But they must preexist. You cannot take an individual image and tell it to move.

■ Keep in mind that the size of an animated GIF file will roughly equal the sum of the sizes of the composite images.

Less is more. The spread of GIF animation skill has led to the spectacle of Web pages littered with winking, blinking, and waving icons. Using animation only for items of central focus will preserve its impact—and will be less likely to annoy the users.

Creating Animated GIFs

We will assume the use of the GIF Construction Set from Alchemy Mindworks, Inc. (Part XV discusses how to acquire the software.) The GIF Construction Set includes an "Animation Wizard" function that will step you through the creation of an animated GIF, with results that are tuned for Web use.

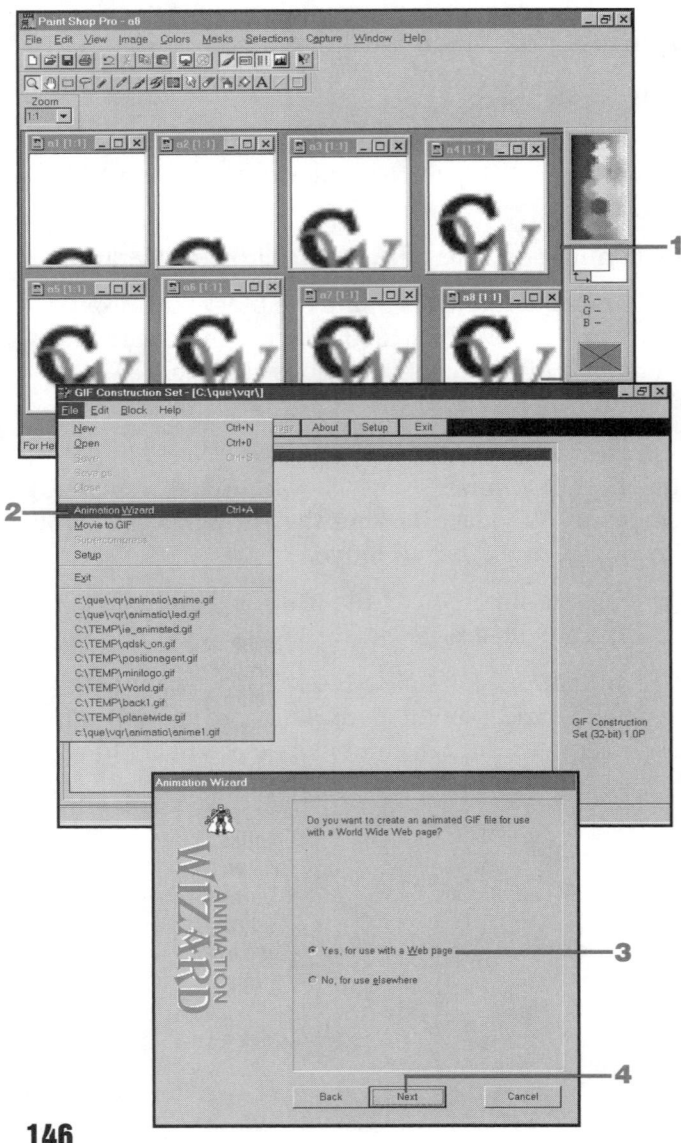

1 Acquire or create a series of GIF images suitable for creating an animation effect. This must precede everything else. Here we'll assume a rising logo, with the motion divided into eight files.

2 Invoke the GIF Construction Set, and under the File command select the Animation Wizard function.

3 After the opening screen, select the Web page option.

4 Click Next.

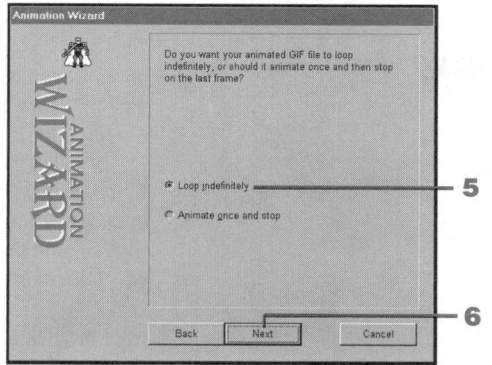

5 On the next screen, select Loop Indefinitely (unless you only want it to loop once after loading).

6 Click Next.

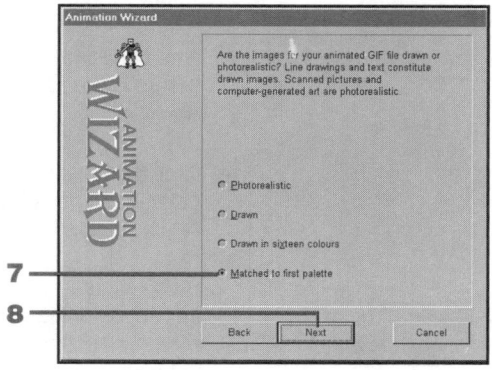

7 On the next screen, select "Matched to First Palette," since they will all be from the same source.

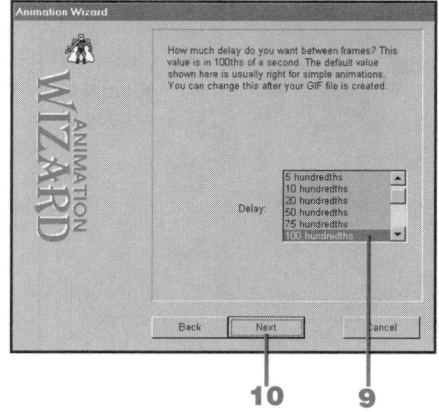

8 Click Next.

9 In the next screen, concerning delays (in hundredths of a second) between frames, select the default option, which will show one frame per second. For smooth, more lifelike animations, you will want a delay of only five-hundredths of a second, but that assumes you also have a long sequence of images.

10 Click Next.

147

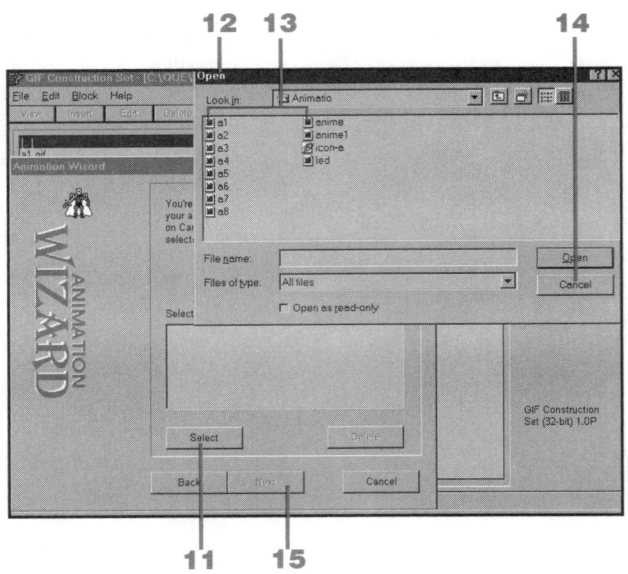

11 In the file selection window that appears, click Select.

12 A file-open window appears. Go to the subdirectory with the images you want to use.

13 Double-click each image you want to use, in the order you want them to appear.

14 When finished, click Cancel in the file-open window.

15 Click Next in the Animation Wizard's file-select window.

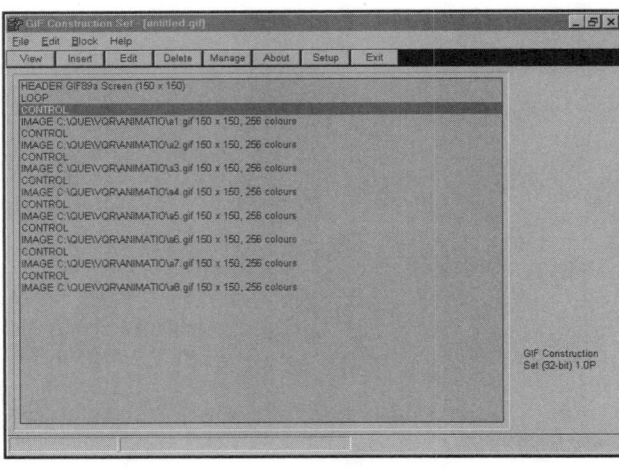

16 Click Done in the next window. GIF Construction Set then processes the files into one set of blocks, as shown.

17 Save the combined file using the File and Save As commands.

18 Add the file to the HTML file of the Web page, as described in Part V.

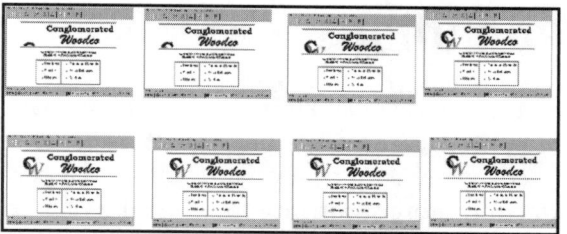

19 Test the file by loading it into your browser while offline, using its load local file command.

The **HEIGHT** and **WIDTH** elements, as well as the **BORDER** element of the **IMG** tag, also work with animations.

Animated GIFs can be linked (using the **<A HREF>** tag) just like any other image, as described in Part VII.

Beware of transparent colors with animations. Although the page's background will show through the transparent background of the image, what may also show through are the "remains" of the previous images in the animation sequence.

Creating Animated Buttons

As you browse the Web, you'll notice the use of small buttons or icons that include animations. These are often used as corporate or product logos, or as variants of an otherwise standard corporate icon that call attention to a particular item. The effect is much subtler and more surprising than the use of a large animation.

And you'll also notice that these buttons pop onto the screen as fast as still buttons. For instance, the Microsoft Internet Explorer logo uses the animated image of a spinning globe with a streak orbiting it. There are 42 images in that animation. Yet, the file is only about 15,000 bytes. This is about nine times larger than a still image of the logo would be (88 pixels by 31 pixels), but still far short of being 42 times longer. The difference is important, since it makes animated buttons a practical way to dress up a page, rather than an impediment to smooth surfing.

You, too, can create your own animated buttons. Let's assume you're using Paint Shop Pro and the GIF Construction Set. We'll also assume you've created the necessary small animation images. That done, proceed as follows.

1 Create a button in Paint Shop Pro, as described in Part IV, but leave enough extra area for the effect you want to add.

2 With the button on the screen, zoomed to a comfortable size, invoke the selection tool.

3 Select an area of the image for the animation images. The readout in the bottom-left corner gives the size of the selected area (18 pixels by 10 pixels, in this case).

4 Note the offset for the top-left corner of the selection: Here it's 24, 3.

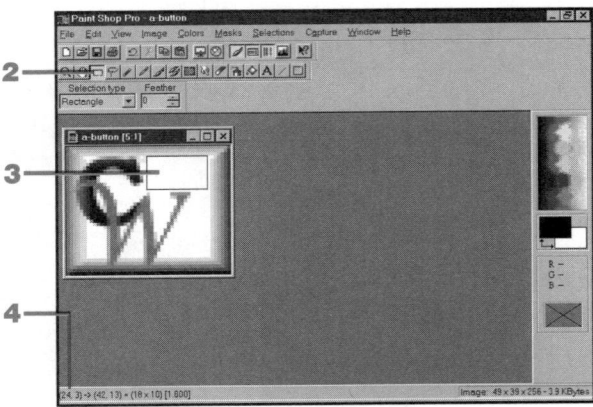

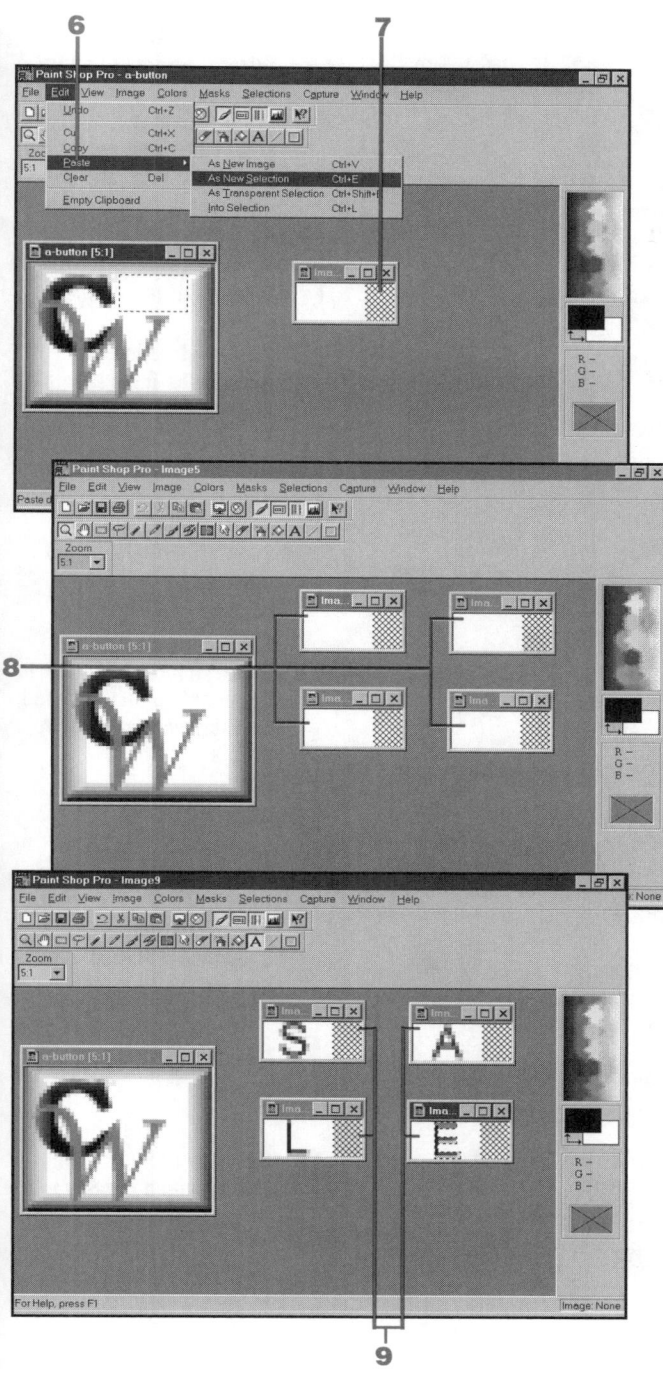

5 Invoke the Edit and Copy commands.

6 Invoke the Edit and then the Paste command, using the As New Selection option.

7 A new image appears, the same size as the selected area in the original image, using its background. Zoom to the same level as the original image.

8 Repeat Steps 6 and 7 as many times as it will take to create the animation you want. (Four times, in this case.)

9 Into each of the new inset images, cut and paste the images from the animation sequence you previously created. (In this case, it's the letters S, A, L, and E, created using the text tool. Creating text with Paint Shop Pro is covered in "Working with Text in an Image" in Part IV.)

10 Save the inset images in the GIF format, presumably with file names numbered sequentially.

11 Open GIF Construction Set.

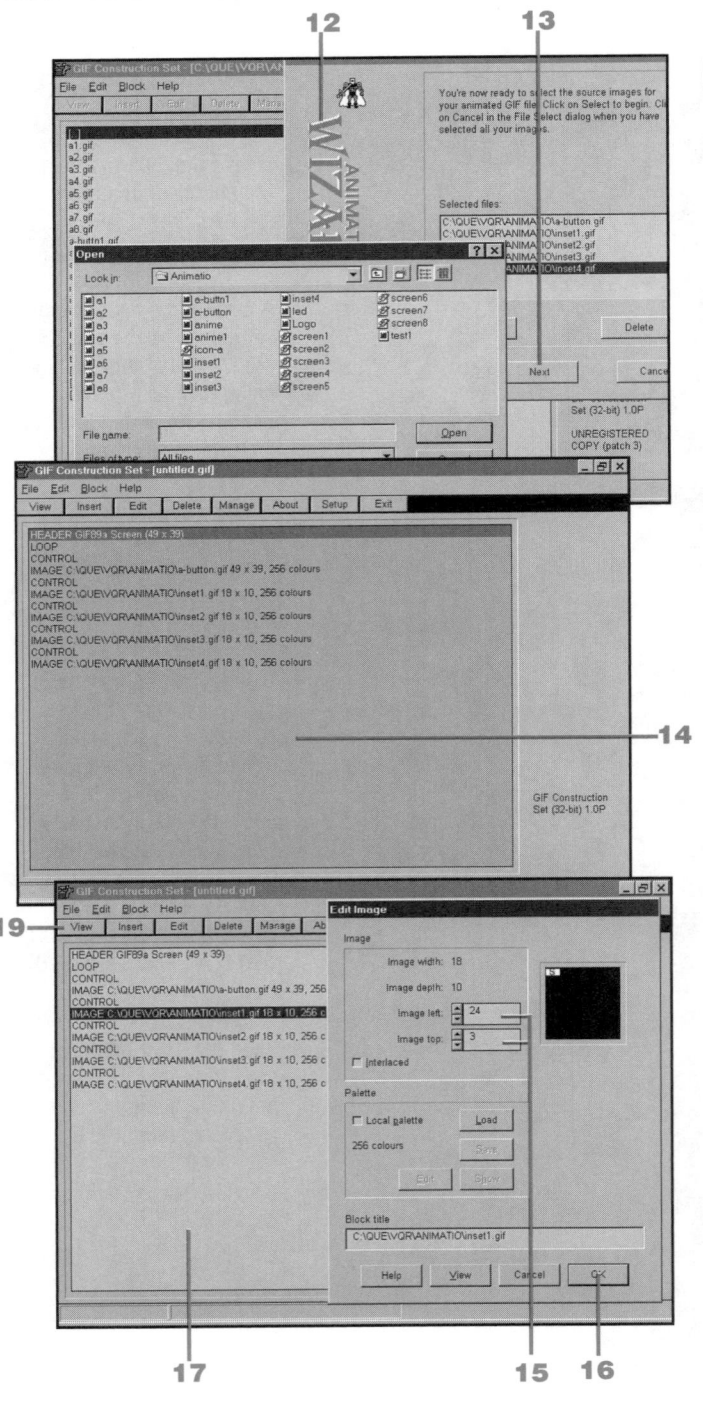

12 Invoke the Animation Wizard, as described in the previous section. When it comes time to select the files, select the button file first, and then the inset files in the animation order.

13 Click Next, then Done.

GIF Construction Set remaps the images into one GIF file, as shown.

14 Double-click the first inset image.

The Edit Image window appears.

15 Set the Image Left and Image Top offset values to the offset value you noted for the selection area in Step 3.

16 Click OK.

You'll see the image in the center of the screen, and the animation sequence will loop over and over.

17 Repeat Steps 14 and 15 for each of the offset images.

18 Save the file using the File and then the Save As command.

19 Test it using the View button.

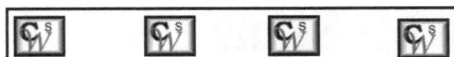

20 **Return from View using the right mouse button.**

21 Further test the file using an offline browser. The GIF file can be loaded directly using the browser's load local file **function.**

22 Add the image to your HTML file as described in Part V.

You usually want to avoid using transparent colors when creating animations.

Each of the inset images should be exactly the same size. Otherwise, momentary fragments of images will litter the picture.

Creating Animated LED Signs

A scrolling marquee effect is a popular addition for Web pages, especially for those associated with the theater, stock market, or Times Square. Since in black and white it also looks like an LED readout, it fits in well with any data processing theme, as shown in our example.

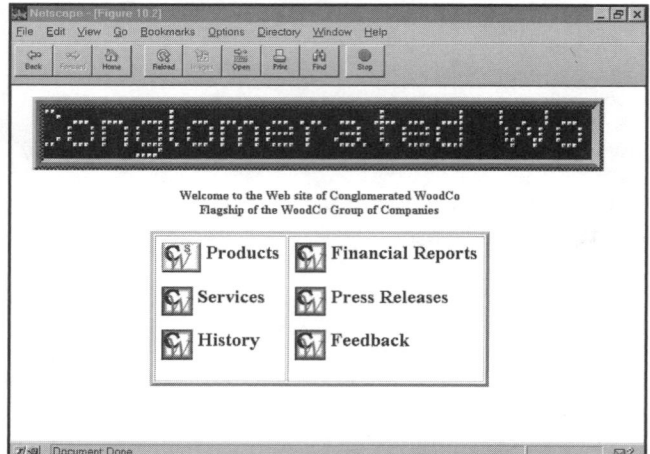

LED sign in use.

Fancy programming is usually required to achieve such an effect, but GIF Construction Set includes a facility for creating such signs. The output is an animated GIF file you can add to your Web page, like any other image file, where it will perform without additional programming.

Keep in mind that this will be an animated GIF file, meaning it will be several times larger than a still GIF. Also, it uses a special set of color codes, shown in Table 10.1. You are limited to these colors.

Table 10.1   LED Color Codes

Code	Example	
Red	@R	@Rletter
Green	@G	@Gpeas
Blue	@B	@Bsea
Cyan	@C	@Csky
Magenta	@M	@Mmountains
Yellow	@Y	@Yleaves
White	@W	@Wlines

You can use as many colors as you like in a sign. (But, as ever, less may be more.) The total length of the message, including the color codes, cannot exceed 260 characters. Any character on your keyboard can be displayed.

Table 10.2 details some of the options available with the LED sign facility.

Table 10.2   LED Sign Options

Option	Note
Loop	The animation cycles only once if this is not checked.
Show Dark Pixels	Sets background LEDs to gray if enabled. This will increase the bytecount of the GIF file.
Smooth Scroll	If enabled, causes the sign to scroll one pixel at a time, rather than one character at a time. This will inflate the bytecount.
Columns per Frame	Sets the smoothness used by the Smooth Scroll option. Adding more columns per frame makes scrolling less smooth, but reduces the file size.
Compact Sign	If checked, the sign will be 40 pixels high; otherwise, it will be 62 pixels high. But you can control image size using the **HEIGHT** element in your HTML file.
Columns Wide	Sets the width of the sign in LED (not pixel) columns.
Delay	Sets the scrolling speed.
Compress palette	If enabled, the file is stored with the least possible color depth.

To create an animated LED sign or marquee with GIF Construction Set, proceed as follows.

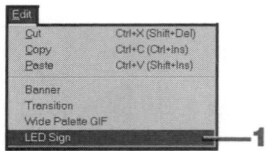

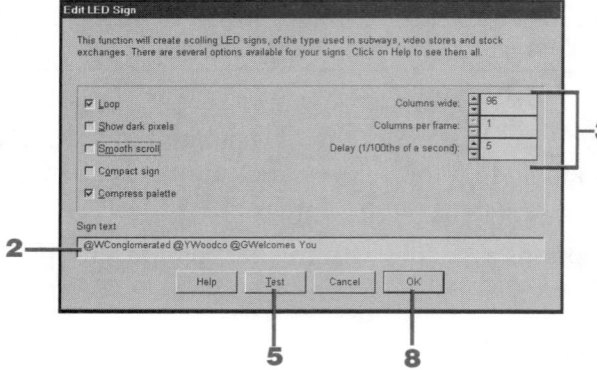

1 In GIF Construction Set, invoke the Edit and then the LED Sign commands. The Edit LED Sign window appears, as shown.

2 Input the Sign Text you want to use, including the color codes.

3 Input the column width you'd like.

4 Change the other settings, according to the chart.

5 Click Test. The scrolling sign is shown on its own screen.

6 Right-click to return to the previous screen.

7 Make any changes to the settings you think appropriate.

8 Click OK. The software then creates the multi-image GIF file, as shown.

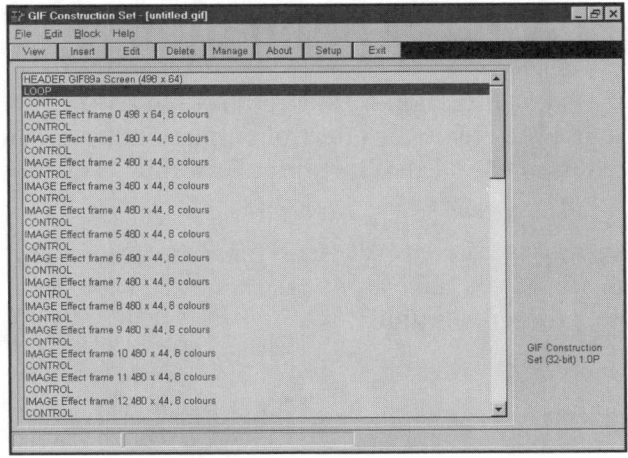

9 Save it in the GIF format using the File and Save As commands.

10 Add the image to the HTML file of the Web page it's being used on, as described in Part V.

11 Test the HTML file by loading it in your browser while offline, using its load local file **function**.

While you can set certain size parameters within the GIF Construction Set for your LED sign, you have ultimate control over its size using the **HEIGHT** element of the **IMG** tag in HTML. (See Part V for details.) Since you'll want the width to change in proportion, the **WIDTH** element is not needed. Our examples show a **HEIGHT** of 120, 90, 75, default, and 20 pixels. Of course, as with any other image, the result will not be usable at all magnifications.

Converting AVI Movies to Animations

The central problem with creating an animation is that you have to have a sequence of images that can be used to create the effect of animation. But plenty of animation clip art (or even live video) exists in computer format. The most common is the AVI format used by Windows.

GIF Construction Set includes a way to convert AVI video files into animated multi-image GIF files automatically. If you have an AVI file that you want to convert to an animated GIF file, proceed as follows.

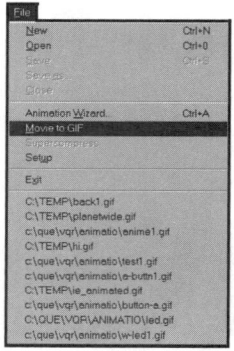

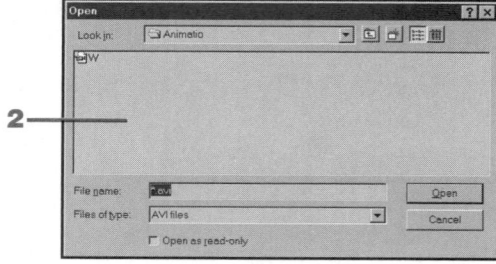

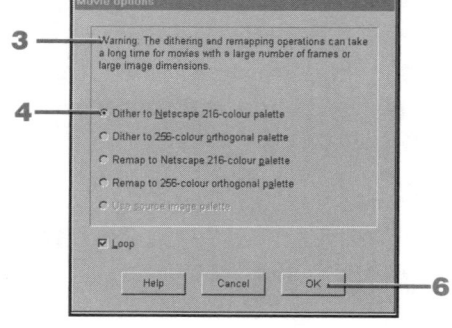

1 In the GIF Construction Set, invoke the File and Movie to GIF commands.

2 The Open window appears. Select the AVI file you want to use by double-clicking it.

3 The Movie Options window appears.

4 In most cases, you will want to use the "Dither to Netscape 216-Color Palette" option. For line drawings, use the "Remap to Netscape 216-Color Palette" option. (Internet Explorer uses the same palette.)

5 Check the Loop option unless you just want the file to run once.

6 Click OK.

The software then creates an image block, with associated control block, for each frame of the AVI file.

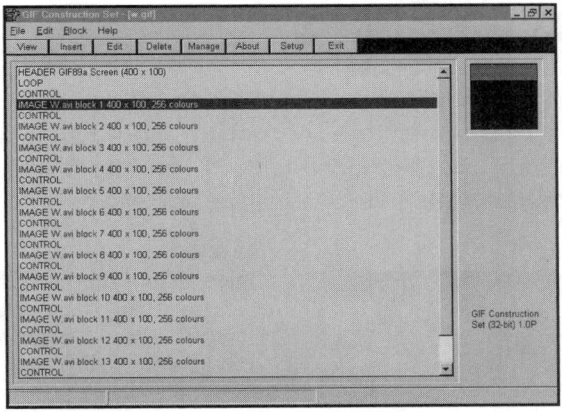

6 Use the File and then the Save As command to save it in the GIF format.

7 Check the file size using File Manager.

8 If it seems too large, remove paired control and image blocks using the Delete button. Since incremental motion is not needed, you can probably remove large but symmetrical chunks—for instance, ten block pairs between each one that you save. However, that depends on the original video and the effect you are trying to achieve.

9 Add the GIF to your Web page's HTML file, as described in Part V.

The GIF files you create from AVI files are likely to be a fraction of the original size of the AVI files. But 10M AVI files are common, and a GIF one-tenth that size is still about 20 times too large for use on a Web page. But jerky motion is usually acceptable for GIF animations, so do not be afraid to trim away image and control blocks.

Multiple Columns on Pages

Left to itself, HTML formats text and other elements so that they flow down the page in one column. Suppose you have three icons each with a short paragraph. Stringing them together gives results like the following example. It looks sloppy, especially the way the text wraps under the icons—a feature you can't control.

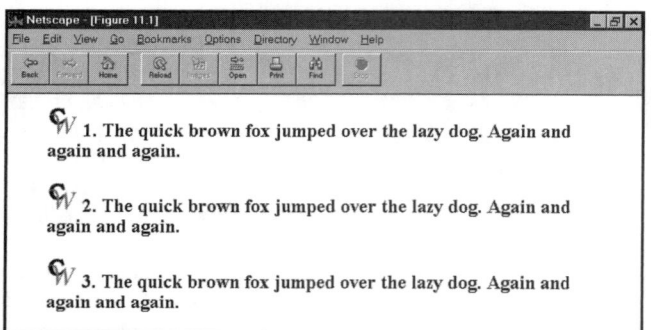

Material formatted without the TABLE function, in one column. There is no way to prevent the text from wrapping under the icon.

A lot of other people didn't like the results either, and evolved the **TABLE** function for HTML. Like a table function in a word processor, it lets you line up material in rows and columns. In our example, you can see that it is the same material as in the first example. But it doesn't exude sloppiness anymore. We have more control over what happens on the page. We can even put lines around paragraphs, pictures, and so on.

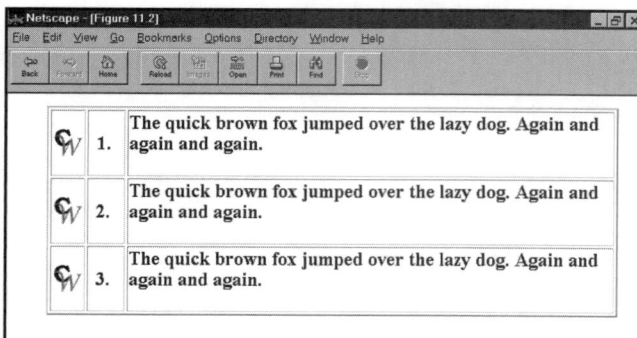

Same material formatted using the TABLE function. Control over the layout is much greater.

Keep in mind that anything can be in the table cells: long paragraphs, single words, images, multiple images, text and images, other tables, and so on. You can use the **TABLE** function to lay out multiple columns on a page, to make sure that pictures and captions align, combine elements, separate elements—it's the Web designer's best friend.

Also keep in mind that you don't have total control over the page's appearance on the screen of a given user. Screen sizes and fonts differ, and earlier browsers don't even support the **TABLE** function. Effects that you labored hours over may be lost to one person, and look like a jumble of screen garbage to someone else.

That said, there are three basic tags in the **TABLE** function (see Table 11.1):

Table 11.1 *TABLE* Tags

Tag	Syntax	Command
<TABLE>	<TABLE>*text*</TABLE>	Material between the tags is defined to be part of a table.
<TR>	<TR>*text*</TR>	Material between the tags is defined as one row of a table.
<TD>	<TD>*text*</TD>	Material between the tags is defined as "table data," i.e., it is the contents of one cell of one row of the table.

The tags must be used in the proper sequence. Individual cell items must be bracketed by the **<TD>** tag. One of more cell items must be bracketed by the **<TR>** tag. Then, the entire block of material is bracketed by the **<TABLE>** tag.

And so, a one-row version of our example would look something like this:

```
<TABLE>
<TR>
<TD><IMG SRC="ICON.GIF"></TD><TD > 1. </TD><TD>The quick brown fox jumped
over the lazy dog. Again and again and again.</TD>
</TR>
</TABLE>
```

The icon, number, and text are divided into three cells using the **<TD>** tags and end tags. That entire line is then made a table row using the **<TR>** tag and end tag. The material as a whole is declared to be a table using the **<TABLE>** tag and end tag. (Incidentally, any spacing and line breaks that enhance legibility of the HTML file are acceptable—the computer just sees is it as one long string of text and code anyway.)

These three tags, however, are only the start. There are elements you can add to the **<TABLE>** and **<TD>** tags to further control the appearance and layout of your material. Our charts examine some of the more common tags. (You can expect new ones to be added as time goes by.)

Typically, you'll want the same number of **<TD>** tags in each row. Otherwise, there may be voids or overhangs in your table. Exceptions include special layout arrangements with the **ROWSPAN** and **COLSPAN** attributes, detailed in Table 11.2, for when you want a cell to span two or more columns (to become a column heading), or when you want a large graphic to occupy a large portion of the table.

Table 11.2 *TABLE* Elements

Element	Syntax	Comment
BORDER	<TABLE BORDER=X>	Puts a border around the table X pixels wide.
WIDTH	<TABLE WIDTH=XX%>	Sizes the table width to XX per cent of the width of the page (when used with the % symbol) or XX number of pixels (when used without the % symbol).
CELLSPACING	<TABLE CELLSPACING=X>	Adds X pixels of space between each cell.
CELLPADDING	<TABLE CELLPADDING=X>	Adds X pixels of space between the cell data and the cell perimeter.
BGCOLOR	<TABLE BGCOLOR="#RGB">	Changes the background of the table to the color specified, using the RGB values or browser-supported names discussed in Part IX.

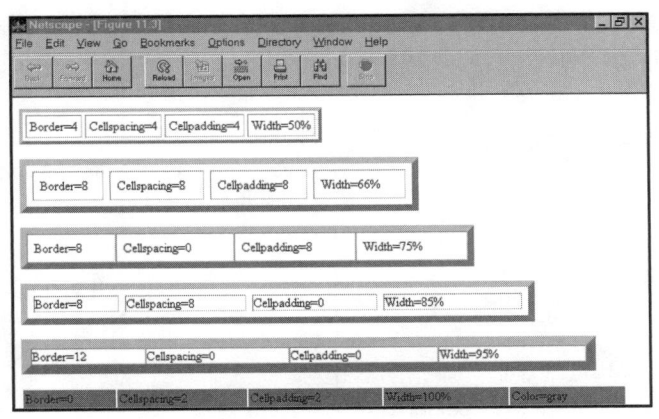

Examples of WIDTH, CELL-PADDING, CELLSPACING, **and background color attributes in use.**

The preceding example shows **TABLE** elements in use. Obviously, it is possible to combine multiple elements in one tag. For instance, the code for the bottom example would be:

<TABLE BORDER=0 CELLPADDING=2 CELLSPACING=2 WIDTH=100% BGCOLOR=GRAY>

Table 11.3 *TD* (Table Data) Attributes

Element	Syntax	Comment
ALIGN	<TD ALIGN=X>	Sets horizontal alignment. X can be **RIGHT**, **LEFT** (default), or **CENTER**.
VALIGN	<TD VALIGN=X>	Sets vertical alignment. X can be **TOP**, **MIDDLE** (default), **BOTTOM**, or **BASELINE**.
ROWSPAN	<TD ROWSPAN=X>	Causes the cell to span X number of rows.
COLSPAN	<TD COLSPAN=X>	Causes the cell to span X number of columns.
NOWRAP	<TD NOWRAP>	Prevents word wrapping inside a cell.
BGCOLOR	<TD BGCOLOR=> "#RGB"	Changes the background of the cell to the color specified, using the **RGB** values or browser-supported names discussed in Part IX.

The **<TR>** tag uses the **ALIGN** and **VALIGN** elements, and can set the default alignment for the cells in that row.

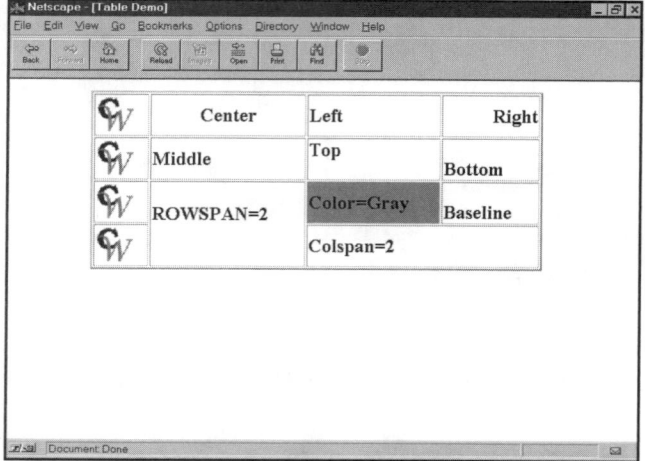

Attributes of the <TD> tag in use, showing what can be done inside table cells.

Displaying Material in Columns (Tables)

To display material in multiple columns using the **TABLE** function, proceed as follows:

```
<IMG SRC="b.gif">Products
<IMG SRC="b.gif">Services
<IMG SRC="b.gif">History
<IMG SRC="b.gif">Financials
<IMG SRC="b.gif">News
<IMG SRC="b.gif">Feedback


<TR>
<IMG SRC="b.gif">Products
<IMG SRC="b.gif">Services
</TR>
<TR>
<IMG SRC="b.gif">History
<IMG SRC="b.gif">Financials
</TR>
<TR>
<IMG SRC="b.gif">News
<IMG SRC="b.gif">Feedback
</TR>


<TR>
<TD><IMG SRC="b.gif"></TD><TD>Products</TD>
<TD><IMG SRC="b.gif"></TD><TD>Services</TD>
</TR>
<TR>
<TD><IMG SRC="b.gif"></TD><TD>History</TD>
<TD><IMG SRC="b.gif"></TD><TD>Financials</TD>
</TR>
<TR>
<TD><IMG SRC="b.gif"></TD><TD>News</TD>
<TD><IMG SRC="b.gif"></TD><TD>Feedback</TD>
</TR>
```

1 Locate the material in the HTML file that you want to display in a table.

2 Decide how many rows you want to have, and divide the material using <TR> tags and end tags. (It's three rows in this case.)

3 Decide how many columns you want. (It should be the same for each row.) Divide the material in that number of columns (two, in this case), using <TD> tags and end tags.

4 Add the <TABLE> tag before and the </TABLE> tags after the material.

165

```
<TABLE>
<TR>
<TD><IMG SRC="b.gif"></TD><TD>Products</TD>
<TD><IMG SRC="b.gif"></TD><TD>Services</TD>
</TR>
<TR>
<TD><IMG SRC="b.gif"></TD><TD>History</TD>
<TD><IMG SRC="b.gif"></TD><TD>Financials</TD>
</TR>
<TR>
<TD><IMG SRC="b.gif"></TD><TD>News</TD>
<TD><IMG SRC="b.gif"></TD><TD>Feedback</TD>
</TR>
</TABLE>
```

5 Save the file in the ASCII text-only format. In some word processors, you may have to close it as well.

6 Test the file by loading it into an offline browser using its load local file function.

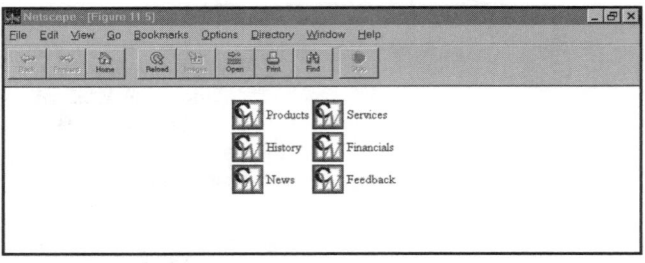

Our table as displayed by a browser.

```
<TABLE BORDER=6 CELLSPACING=
4 WIDTH=50% CELLPADDING=4>
<TR ALIGN=CENTER>
<TD><IMG SRC="b.gif"></TD><TD>Products</TD>
<TD><IMG SRC="b.gif"></TD><TD>Services</TD>
</TR>
<TR ALIGN=CENTER>
<TD><IMG SRC="b.gif"></TD><TD>History</TD><TD>
<IMG SRC="b.gif"></TD><TD>Financials</TD>
</TR>
<TR ALIGN=CENTER>
<TD><IMG SRC="b.gif"></TD><TD>News</TD>
<TD><IMG SRC="b.gif"></TD><TD>Feedback</TD>
</TR>
</TABLE>
```

7 Add elements from the chart that you think might make the layout more appealing. (In this case: BORDER, WIDTH, CELLSPACING, and CELLPADDING for the TABLE element, and ALIGN for the TR tag.)

8 Again, save the file in the ASCII text-only format.

9 Again, test it using an offline browser.

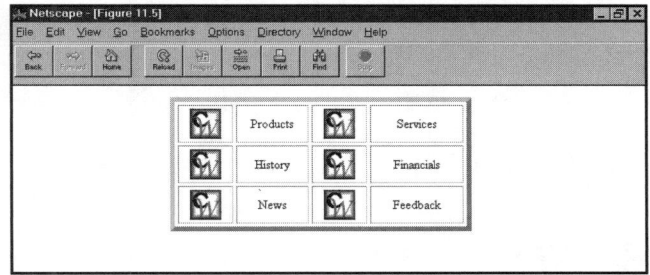

Our finished table, spruced up with border, spacing, and alignment features.

By putting GIF images with transparent backgrounds inside the cells of a borderless table, you can create impressive artistic effects, logos, collages, and navigation helpers. The **TABLE** function can also let you position multiple small images to create the effect of one large image.

```
<TABLE BORDER=6 CELLSPACING=4 WIDTH=50%
CELLPADDING=4>
<TR ALIGN=CENTER VALIGN=MIDDLE>
<TD><A HREF="a.htm"><IMG SRC="b.gif"></A></TD>
<TD><A HREF="a.htm">Products</A></TD>
<TD><A HREF="b.htm"><IMG SRC="b.gif"></A></TD>
<TD><A HREF="b.htm">Services</A></TD>
</TR>
<TR ALIGN=CENTER>
<TD><A HREF="c.htm"><IMG SRC="b.gif"></A></TD>
<TD><A HREF="c.htm">History</A></TD>
<TD><A HREF="d.htm"><IMG SRC="b.gif"></A></TD>
<TD><A HREF="d.htm">Financials</A></TD>
</TR>
<TR ALIGN=CENTER>
<TD><A HREF="e.htm"><IMG SRC="b.gif"></A></TD>
<TD><A HREF="e.htm">News</A></TD>
<TD><A HREF="f.htm"><IMG SRC="b.gif"></A></TD>
<TD><A HREF="f.htm">Feedback</A></TD>
</TR>
</TABLE>
```

10 Add any further embellishments the file needs, such as hyperlink tags.

11 Continue altering and testing the code until you get the layout you want.

We have changed the format of the HTML code, which you can always do to improve legibility—the computer does not care.

If you are linking items inside a table cell, the link does not extend beyond the cell. If, for instance, you want to link all the items in a table to the same page, you will have to add an anchor tag to each cell.

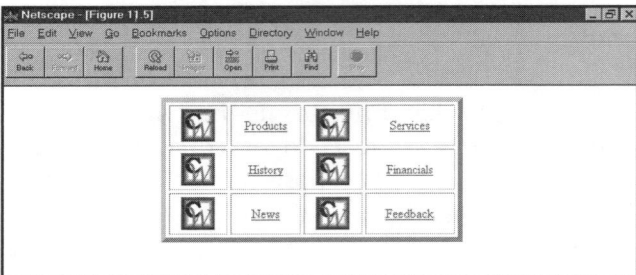

The demo table with links added to the text and images. The image borders could be removed using the BORDER element of the IMG tag.

Using Frames with Pages

The **FRAME** function takes the **TABLE** function one step farther. Not only can you divide up the page into columns and rows, you can divide the browser window into a collection of separate HTML files each in their own window. In fact, the contents of each frame must be a full and complete HTML file, and each can have its own background, color scheme, layout, and so on. The material is formatted using the available space in the frame and, optionally, scroll bars can be added if content won't fit in the frame's window.

There are many things you can do with frames, but we will concern ourselves only with the (very popular) use demonstrated by our example. Its layout answers two basic concerns. First, you'd like to use your corporate logo and color scheme in the background, but it degrades the legibility of the text. Secondly, you'd like to keep your site's table of contents constantly in view.

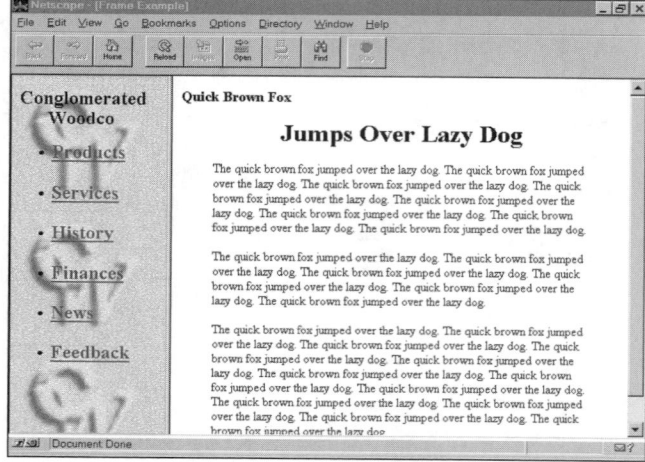

Page laid out with two frames.

Our two-column frame layout lets you keep the table of contents on the left at all times. You can use your colors and backgrounds there, where it won't cause headaches. The main window on the right contains the actual reading material. Clicking the linked items in the contents screen will cause those pages to appear in the right side window.

A Web page with frames has only two operative tags: **FRAMESET** and **FRAME**. The **<FRAMESET>** sets up the number of rows and columns that will appear on the page. Between **<FRAMESET>** and its **</FRAMESET>** end tag is a **<FRAME>** tag for each frame created by **<FRAMESET>**, setting the characteristics of that frame. Elements used in each are shown in the tables that follow. The operative code of our example (not counting the files displayed in the frames) is only four lines:

```
<FRAMESET COLS="*, 3*">
<FRAME SRC="toc.htm" NAME="side">
<FRAME SRC="hello.htm" NAME="main">
</FRAMESET>
```

There is another tag you'll need to know about that is not strictly a **FRAME** tag: **<NOFRAMES>**. You use this tag to designate the part of the HTML file that will be used by browsers that do not support the **FRAME** tag (see Table 12.1).

Table 12.1   Elements of the *FRAMESET* Tag

FRAMESET Elements	Comments
ROWS="X, Y, …"	The comma-separated values set the relative size of the rows. You can use percentages, such as "25%, 25%, 50%." Or you can use relative values, where an asterisk represents the smallest frame and the others are multiples of it: "*, *, 2*." The browser will calculate the actual size of each frame. Or you can use actual pixel widths: "100, 100, 200." You can even combine the methods. But there must be a value for each row created.
COLS="X, Y, …"	Sets column values, assigned as above.

Table 12.2 shows elements of the **FRAME** tag.

Table 12.2   Elements of the *FRAME* Tag

FRAME Elements	Comments
SRC="file"	Name of the HTML file that will fill that frame.
NORESIZE	Keeps the users from resizing the frame, which they can normally do. (If one frame on a page cannot be resized, the others cannot either.)
SCROLLING=X	X can be YES, NO, or AUTO (the default). YES adds a scroll bar to the frame regardless of whether it needs one. NO prevents a scroll bar from ever appearing. AUTO means one will be added if the material cannot otherwise fit the frame.
NAME="X"	X can be any word. It assigns a name to that frame for the browser's internal use.
MARGINWIDTH="X"	Adds X pixels between the right and left sides of a frame and the content of the frame.
MARGINHEIGHT="X"	Adds X pixels between the top and bottom boundaries of the frame and the content of the frames.

There must be no **<BODY>** tag on a page with frames. The browser will go blank. (It can be in the **<NOFRAMES>** portion.)

Creating Frame-Based Pages

To create a Web page (or entire site) based on frames, unified by a table of contents frame as in the previous example, proceed as follows.

1. Create your site without frames.

2. Open the HTML file that serves as the opening page of the site and locate the **<BODY>** tag.

   ```
   <BODY>
   ```

3. Insert the **<NOFRAMES>** tag above it, and the **</NOFRAMES** end tag at the end of the file. The material between them—your original Web page—will be displayed by browsers that cannot display frames.

   ```
   <NOFRAMES>
   <BODY>
   ...
   </BODY>
   </NOFRAMES>
   ```

4. Above the **<NOFRAMES>** tag insert the **<FRAMESET>** tag, with **ROWS** and **COLS** elements as described in the previous section, together creating the number of frames you want.

   ```
   <FRAMESET COLS="*, 3*">
   <NOFRAMES>
   <BODY>
   ...
   </BODY>
   </NOFRAMES>
   ```

5. Below **<FRAMESET>** insert a **<FRAME>** tag for each frame created by **<FRAMESET>**. You must include the **SRC** element. For our example to work, you must also use the **NAME** element.

   ```
   <FRAMESET COLS="*, 3*">
   <FRAME SRC="toc.htm" NAME="side">
   <FRAME SRC="hello.htm" NAME="main">
   <NOFRAMES>
   <BODY>
   ...
   </BODY>
   </NOFRAMES>
   ```

6. Insert the **</FRAMESET>** end-tag.

```
<FRAMESET COLS="*, 3*">
<FRAME SRC="toc.htm" NAME="side">
<FRAME SRC="hello.htm" NAME="main">
</FRAMESET>
<NOFRAMES>
<BODY>
...
</BODY>
</NOFRAMES>
```

7. Save the file in the ASCII text-only format using the .htm extension.

8. Create an HTML file, as described in Parts V and VI, and so on, to serve as the table of contents.

Any images that are intended for use in **FRAMESRC** HTML files should be resized to fit the expected size of the frame using the methods described in Part III.

9. The **TARGET** element should be added to the anchor tags of the links that comprise the table of contents frame. When clicked, the file that is being called up will be displayed in the frame carrying the name used by the **TARGET** element.

```
<A HREF="prods.htm" TARGET="main">Products</A>
```

10. Save the file.

11. Test both files using an offline browser.

You can create any number of frames on a page, but if you want to go beyond four, you are probably wiser to use the **TABLE** function, described in Part IX.

Using Images with Frames

When using images with frames (which we did not do in the previous section, except in the background), you run into a problem: An individual image may easily be larger than the frame that is supposed to contain it. The browser responds by displaying whatever corner of the image it can fit into the frame, and adding scroll bars to get at the rest, as in our example.

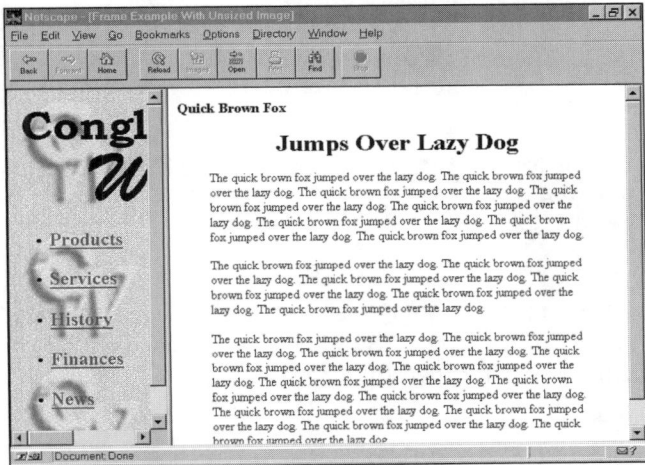

The corporate logo is too large to fit inside the index frame, so the browser has added scroll bars and shown one corner of it.

The resulting effect may be something that you just have to put up with (as in a large map). Or you may actually like it. Chances are, you'll hate it. And you'll be relieved to know it is avoidable, thanks to two HTML features:

- The **WIDTH** and **HEIGHT** attributes of the **IMG** tag, as detailed in Part V. (We'll only use the **WIDTH** control, since the **HEIGHT** will automatically be proportionate.)

- The pixel width control possible with the **FRAMESET** tag, as detailed in the beginning of (this) Part XII.

Basically, you set the pixel width of the frame that will hold the image, and then add the **WIDTH** element to the image's **IMG** tag to ensure that it will fit.

To create a Web page based on frames, with fitted graphics, proceed as follows:

1. Create the page as described in the previous section.

2. In the main or index file that contains the **FRAMESET** tag, locate the **FRAMESET** tag.

   ```
   <FRAMESET COLS="*, 3*">
   ```

3. Change the **COLS** element (or **ROW** element, if used) of the frame with the image to reflect an exact pixel size. In this case, the first column has the image, and we'll set it to 170 pixels. (The second column can be represented by an *, and it will take up the rest of the window.)

   ```
   <FRAMESET COLS="170, *">
   ```

4. In the HTML of the file that is loaded into that frame by the **FRAME** tag, locate the **IMG** tag of the image.

   ```
   <IMG SRC=logo.gif>
   ```

5. Add a **WIDTH** element to the tag so the image is slightly smaller than the width we just assigned to the frame in the **FRAMESET** tag. Since we set the frame to 170 pixels, we will set the image **WIDTH** to 140 pixels.

   ```
   <IMG SRC=logo.gif WIDTH=150>s
   ```

6. Save both files in the ASCII text-only format using the .htm extension. In some word processors, you may have to close them as well.

7. Test them with an offline browser.

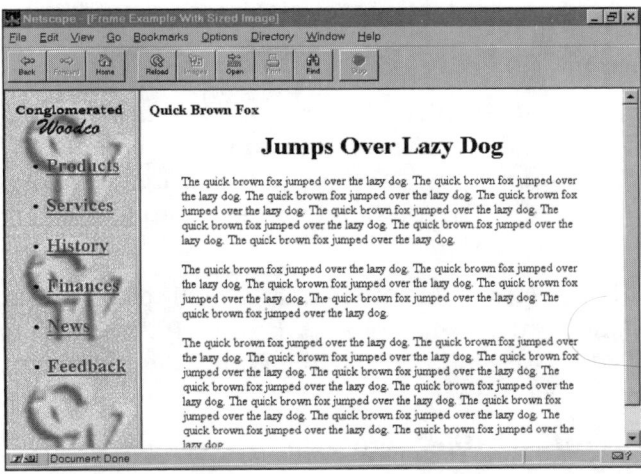

Frames-based page with
the logo sized to fit the
index frame.

Working with Photos

This book emphasizes the creation of graphical elements using common graphics software. But you will often want to use photos on your page. These, of course, you must capture using photographic equipment. If you are not using a digital camera, or if the image already exists on film (as is usually the case), you will have to scan it to make a digital version.

Which brings us to the world of electronic imaging—a large field served by an expanding corps of full-time, dedicated professionals, whose craft demands mastery of a large body of knowledge. We can't replicate the knowledge here, but there are some basic tips that can guide you:

- **Scan from slides, if at all possible.** With slides, you can have about twice the contrast possible with the printed page—contrast that is a closer match to that of a computer screen. But the equipment is expensive, and you will probably have to go through a commercial service bureau. But if the image exists only as a print, you will have to use a flatbed scanner.

- **Avoid halftone images.** Images from printed books, magazines, and newspapers can be counted on to produce unwanted background patterns (called "moires") when scanned. Basically, you are better off getting the original photo from the source (which also implies that you have permission to reproduce it and are not violating any copyright laws). Otherwise, you might try scanning it at a higher resolution than you need, and then reducing it using the resize command. (Use Image/Resize in Paint Shop Pro.) You can also try using image filters that will "despeckle" or soften the image. (In Paint Shop Pro, try Image/Normal Filters/Soften, and Image/Special Filters/Despeckle.) Paradoxically, adding noise (random dots) to the image may also help. (In Paint Shop Pro, use Image/Special Filters/Add Noise.)

- **Watch your file sizes.** Color photos can produce large files. Size can be controlled by resizing, cropping, and by paying attention to color depth, as described in Part III.

- **Use high resolutions with line art.** Line art, when scanned at a one to one resolution, generally produces jagged edges on curves. Try using a higher resolution and then resizing. Scanning line art as a grayscale image is usually a mistake (unless it is, for instance, a pencil sketch with lots of shading). Meanwhile, auto-trace features available on various graphics programs (which create a vector image that can be resized without creating jagged-edge distortions) generally are practical only for very simple images.

- **Try 1:1 resolution with grayscale.** Grayscale images usually give better results if scanned at close to one-to-one resolution and then sharpened using filters in the graphics program. In Paint Shop Pro, try Image/Normal Filters/Sharpen.

- **Cropping—don't be afraid to do it.** White borders, even if you are making them disappear using the transparent color function, still require space in the file. In fact, with transparent backgrounds you have even less need for borders. Cropping is covered in Part III.

- **Always test the image.** What it looks like on the browser screen is the final judge.

Graphics software and scanner/cameras that support the TWAIN standard can work together automatically. For instance, after scanning, you can use the File/Acquire command in Paint Shop Pro to access the scanned images. (If more than one TWAIN device is installed, you may have to use the File/Select Source command first.) And, yes, TWAIN is *said* to stand for Technology Without An Interesting Name.

Color and Palettes

Many users have monitors limited to the display of 256 colors. The leading Web browsers use a palette of 216 colors that are (from the original 256) shared by the Windows and Macintosh systems.

Color imagery is the passion of a corps of professionals who depend on a considerable fund of knowledge and skill, and this book is not in a position to turn you into a graphics artist. However, you can proceed with confidence by keeping these points in mind:

- Whatever its color depth, most images can be shown using 216 colors.

- Most photographs look fine with dithered colors, since the beholder, who is not living inside a cartoon, expects the color to change from one spot to the next.

- Images with large fields of solid color may not look so good when dithered, since the dithering may end up looking like speckling—the image will look dirty where you want it to look smooth.

The answer to the last problem is to create the image using a color palette designed for Web use, using the 216-color browser palette. These "Web safe" palettes are available for downloading on numerous Web sites, such as at **www.lynda.com/hex.html**.

To use a Web safe palette, proceed as follows:

1. Download one of the "Web safe" color images. When you see it on the screen, you can do so by clicking it using the right mouse button.

2. Load it into Paint Shop Pro the usual way.

3. After you have it on the screen, select the Colors and then the Save Palette commands. The software then composes a palette composed of the colors contained in the image.

4. The software will ask you to name the file it is creating. Select a reasonable name: web.pal, for instance. Then click Save.

5. When editing the image, load the Web palette you saved by using the Colors and then the Load Palette commands.

Your image will be limited to the "native colors" of the Web, and no dithering will occur on either Macintosh or Windows platforms. Part III discusses color depth and how to change it.

Using Thumbnails

Although using small images is generally the best policy on the Web, there are images that you will want to use full-size. Maps, schematics, and detailed photos of parts convey important information and should not be resized for aesthetic reasons. If the user has to scroll around inside the image, fine.

The procedure commonly used is to put a large image on a page by itself. Then you link to that page from a main page using a thumbnail—a smaller version of the large image, one that fits on the main page and adds minimally to the page's download time. The link should clearly state the size of the image, so those with slower modems can elect not to get tied up with it.

Unless there is one striking element of the original image whose impact you want to convey (such as the dancing eyes of the model holding the product), it is usually better to resize the image rather than crop it.

If you are resizing, it is better to create a second, smaller version of the image than to depend on the **HEIGHT** or **WIDTH** resizing elements of the **IMG** tag (discussed in Part V). Graphics software usually does a better job of image manipulation than a browser.

To use a thumbnail image on a Web page, proceed as follows.

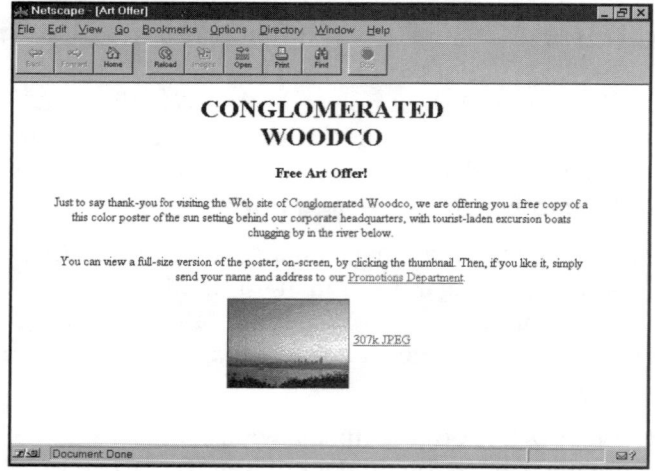

1. Decide whether you want to crop the original image or resize it.

2. Crop or resize the image, as detailed in Part III, saving it under a new file name.

3. Add the new image to your HTML page, as described in Part V.

4. Create an HTML page that contains only the original, large image.

5. Link the thumbnail image to the new page with the large image, as detailed in Part VII.

6. Add file size information about the large image to the caption of the thumbnail image, as in our examples.

Paint Shop Pro also includes a feature called thumbnails, which you can use to select what image you want to edit. Using the File, Browse commands, you can choose a directory to examine, and then Paint Shop Pro will present thumbnail versions of every image file in that directory. Clicking a thumbnail will load that image for editing.

Mounting Files on the Web

As noted in Part I, the Web is a subset of the Internet, a global affiliation of computers, connected by high-speed links, that responds to a standard set of commands.

The upshot is that the presence of your Web files in your desktop machine does not mean they are on the Web, regardless of whether you are connected to the Web. For them to be part of the Web, they must be stored on a Web server. To accomplish this task, there are two things you will need:

- A Web site where you can mount the files, which usually means rented space on the Web server of a Web presence provider.

- Web access by which you can view and check the files, which usually means a subscription with a Web access provider.

And it means you will need a desktop computer with browser software and a high-speed modem, like any other Web surfer.

The Web presence provider and the Web access provider can be the same firm, often called an Internet Service Provider (ISP).

And, generally, you can expect to get an Internet access account (plus an e-mail address) with a Web presence account.

However, the access provider and the Web presence provider need not be the same firm. The Web site, the sponsoring organization, and the Web designer can be in three different cities— if not three different continents—and it will make no difference.

But assuming you've arranged for a Web site and for Web access, there are two things left to consider:

- File-naming questions must be settled.

- The files must get transmitted to the server.

We'll cover each in detail in the following sections.

File Name Considerations

When acquiring a Web site through an ISP or any other Web service, the first thing you need to do is settle file-naming considerations. In other words:

■ Is the server case-sensitive with file names?

■ Does the server require the .html or .htm extension for HTML files?

As for the first consideration, "case-sensitive" means that logo.gif, LOGO.GIF, and, for that matter, Logo.Gif are different file names. (In other words, the computer sees uppercase and lowercase letters as unrelated symbols.) And it is standard for server software to be case-sensitive. So there are two things you need to do:

1. While creating the Web files, make sure you are using a consistent file name style: sticking to lowercase is the best bet.

2. After the files are loaded, check to see if file names match the style you used—uppercase or lowercase. Even if you consistently used lowercase names, file names will sometimes get converted to uppercase when handled by older PC software.

As for the second consideration, many Web servers run some version of the UNIX operating system, which allows four-letter extensions. It may be that the server expects HTML files to have the full .html extension. (The extensions of the other common Web formats—IF, JPG, and PNG—should not be an issue, since they are called from within the HTML files.)

If this is the case, the staff of the ISP may have a facility for telling the server to treat the .htm extension as if it were the .html extension.

Otherwise, the .html extension is required, and there are two things you will have to do:

1. You will have to make special versions of your files before you upload them to the server. When you wrote them originally, you used the .htm extension so you could test the links on a Windows machine. You will need to load each into a word processor and do a search-replace, converting each instance of .htm into .html.

2. Once uploaded to the server, you will have to rename each HTML file, changing the extension of .htm (which it inherited from your Windows machine) to .html. The commands needed to do this will depend on the configuration of your ISP's systems, and you will have to get specific directions from the staff.

Transmission Methods

Once finished, your Web files must be mounted on a server of the Internet Service Provider (ISP) where you have a Web site, as explained in the previous sections. This means transmitting them to the server where they will be copied into the public-access subdirectory that corresponds to your Web site, according to the internal addressing scheme of that server.

And the details of how you will go about this will differ with each server and ISP. There is no getting around it—you will have to ask them for directions. Don't be shy. They've heard these questions before and probably have printed instructions.

However, the most common approach involves using the FTP (File Transfer Protocol), an Internet facility that is also included in Windows 95 (see Table 14.1). If you have your files finished, have your Web access and Web presence accounts, have the FTP address that your ISP uses for Web sites (ask the staff for it), and have the name and password used for the account.

If you forget the bin command, any image files you transmit will be corrupted. HTML files, however, will arrive intact. (They're text, not binary files.)

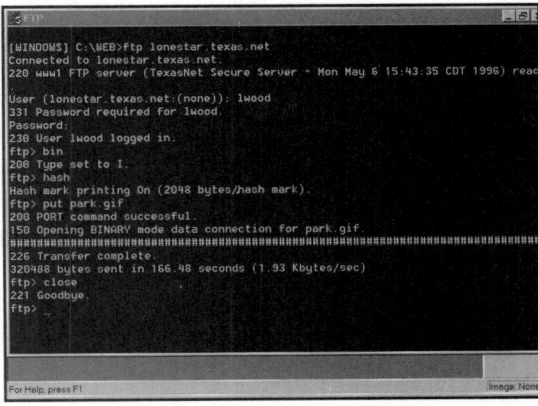

1 Go online with your browser in the usual fashion.

2 Invoke the Programs command, and click the MS-DOS Prompt option.

3 After the MS-DOS window appears, navigate to the directory that contains the files you want to upload.

4 Type: FTP *XXXX* where *XXXX* is the FTP address used by your ISP for Web site accounts.

5 When asked for a name, give the user name assigned to the Web site accounts, and press Enter.

6 When asked for a password, give the password assigned to that Web site account, and press Enter.

7 You will then have access to the directory on the server assigned to your Web site. You can perform the FTP commands shown in the chart. Typically, you will start with the bin and hash commands, and then use put or mput to transmit the files. Then ls or dir can be used to verify their arrival.

8 When finished, use the quit command to end the FTP session.

9 Input Exit to leave MS-DOS and return to Windows.

Table 14.1 FTP Commands

Command	Syntax	Comment
bin	bin	Binary Mode, for sending everything but text
ls	ls	Lists the files in directory giving names only
put	put xxx.htm	Transmits the named file from your machine to the server
mput	mput *.htm	Multi-file put command. You will be queried for each file matching the wild card.
get	get xxx.htm	Triggers the transmission of the named file to your machine
mget	mget *.htm	Multi-file get command. You will be queried for each file matching the wild card.
dir	dir	Lists the files named in the directory, giving sizes, dates, and so on
cd	cd /dirname	Change directory—works as in DOS
close	close	Closes your connection with the FTP site, but the FTP software remains loaded
quit	quit	Ends the FTP program and returns you to DOS
hash	hash	Outputs hash marks at intervals during a file transmission so you'll be assured something is happening

This section should be seen as an example. Logon procedures may vary, and not all commands in the chart may be implemented the same way—or at all—by an ISP. Get directions from your vendor.

If, after transmitting files, you need to rename or delete some of them, you can input the necessary commands to the server using the Telnet command. Like FTP, Telnet is an Internet facility that is included in Windows 95, and can be invoked from the DOS prompt or the File Manager. (It's in the Windows directory.) But, once logged on, the commands you will need vary from ISP to ISP, so you will need to get directions.

Web Graphics Tools and Sources

In this book, we have emphasized tools that you probably either already possess or ones that can be acquired over the Web itself. Basically, with a fast modem, you can be fully equipped and on your way in an hour. The following tools will be enough to make you productive on the Web:

- Notepad (for writing HTML files)
- Paint Shop Pro (for processing images)
- A browser (for testing)
- GIF Construction Set, if you are doing animations

Of course, there are other tools for special purposes, and a number of graphics packages that you might already have can do the same job as Paint Shop Pro. Our Online Sources chart (see Table 15.1) shows the tools available for downloading, and the Commercial Sources chart (see Table 15.2) shows popular alternatives.

Table 15.1   Online Sources

Name	URL	Retail	Comment
Paint Shop Pro	**www.jasc.com**	$69.00	All-round tool with features aimed at Web graphics.
GIF Construction Set	**www.mindworkshop .com**	$25.00	Simple yet powerful GIF animation tool.
Live Image	**www.mediatec.com**	$29.95	Turns images into image maps.
Windows FTP	In Windows 95, use Start, Run, C:\WINDOWS\FTP.EXE	Part of Windows 95	Internet File Transfer Protocol.
Color Manipulation	**www.meat.com/ software/cmd.html**	$15.00	Preview background Device and text color by RGB value. Can also preview background images.

Table 15.2   Commercial Sources

Name	URL	Retail	Comment
Corel Photo-Paint	**www.corel.ca**	$495	Graphics program with animations, transparency, image-map creation, PNG port.
Photo Shop	**www.adobe.com**	$895	Professional-level features. Numerous filters and color control tools. Supports PNG. Has Windows, Macintosh, and UNIX versions.

Remember to pay for the shareware programs you acquire, especially if you are going to use their output online. Paying helps support the shareware industry and promotes the availability of such software—offering you, for trivial sums, functionality that would have cost thousands of dollars a few years ago. Also, unregistered copies of some programs (such as GIF Construction Set) may place comments in your files that you may not notice but which the software vendors can find using search engines.

Most online software is also available at "mirror sites" which collect material offered by other sites. When looking for Web tools, good mirror site bets would be the SimTel site at **www.coast.net/SimTel**, and the TUCOWS site at **www.tucows.com**.

How to Download

When online with your browser, when you click a file that the browser cannot format, run, or otherwise figure out what to do with, it asks you how to proceed. One of the options it gives you will be to save the file to disk.

And that is how you download software from the Web. You go to the URL of the vendor (or mirror site), follow the links to the download file, click it, and save it to disk.

Then, you go offline to install it to disk. Usually, it will be in a self-extracting file that will decompress itself into the composite files of the package and install it in an appropriate subdirectory, and even add itself to your Start menu. Then, you can delete the original download file.

As an example, proceed as follows:

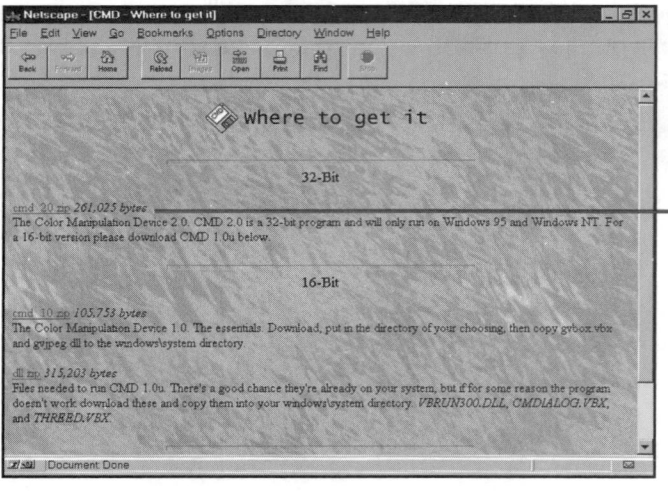

1 Locate the download file at the Web site in question, as shown here.

2 Click it. The Unknown File Type window will appear.

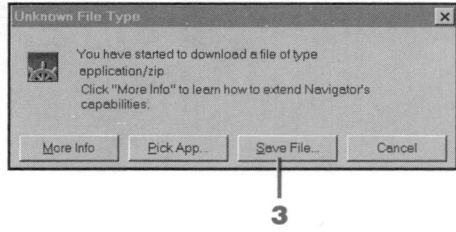

3 Click the Save File Button.

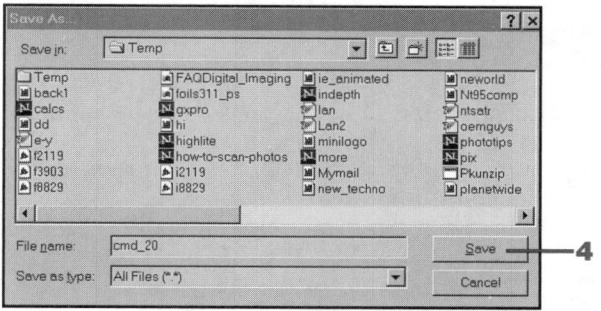

4 Click Save. The Save As window appears. You probably do not need to change the name, but note the sub-directory where the file is being stored.

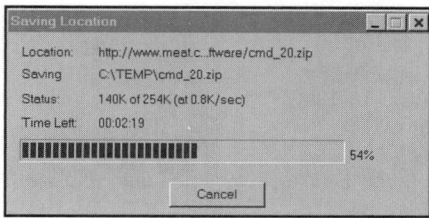

5 The Saving Location window appears showing the progress of the download. After progress reaches 100%, the window disappears. Go offline and proceed as follows.

If the file has the .exe extension, that means it is a self-extracting compressed archive:

1. Open your File Manager program.

2. Find the file you just downloaded.

3. Double-click it.

4. It should decompress and install itself.

If the file has the .zip extension, it is a compressed archive in the ZIP format:

1. If you do not have pkunzip, download it from **www.pkware.com**, as described in the previous section. It is self-extracting.

2. Put the resulting pkunzip.exe and the downloaded ZIP file in the same sub-directory.

3. In File Manager, invoke File, Run, and input pkunzip.exe *.zip.

4. After decompression, look for a README file with installation instructions.

Index

A

A NAME tags, 118
A tags, 117
   HREF attribute, 119
   NAME attribute, 119, 122
   TARGET attribute, 119
ALIGN attribute
   IMG tag, 77-79
   TD tags, 163
ALT attribute, IMG tag, 75
animations
   animated buttons,
     150-153
   AVI movies, 158-159
   GIF files, 144-148
     links, 149
     looping, 147
   LED marquees, 154-157
AREA tags, 132
aspect ratio of resized
  graphics, 33
attributes
   A tag
     HREF, 119
     NAME, 119, 122
     TARGET, 119
   BODY tags
     BACKGROUND,
      142-143
     BGCOLOR, 138-139
   FONT tag
     COLOR, 101-103
     FACE, 98-100
     formatting options,
      104-106
   IMG SRC tags, 132
   IMG tag, 73
     ALIGN, 77-79
     ALT, 75
     BORDER, 76, 126
     HEIGHT, 80-81
     HSPACE, 83
     LOWSRC, 84-86
     VSPACE, 82
     WIDTH, 80-81

   TABLE tags, 162
   TD tags, 163
   text styles, 91
AVI movies as animations,
  158-159

B

BACKGROUND attribute,
  BODY tags, 142-143
backgrounds, Web pages,
  134-139, 142-143
BGCOLOR attribute
   BODY tags, 138-139
   TABLE tags, 162
   TD tags, 163
blurring options for drop-
  shadow buttons, 47
BMP file conversions
   GIF, 17-18
   PNG, 24-25
BODY tags, 72
   BACKGROUND attribute,
     142-143
   BGCOLOR attribute,
     138-139
BORDER attribute
   IMG tags, 76, 126
   TABLE tags, 162
borders, removing from
  linked graphics, 125-126
BR (break) function, 67
BR tags, 89
browsers, 2
   checking image file con-
     versions, 31
   see also Web browsers
bullets in lists, 111-112
buttons, 40, 43-44, 150-153

C

CELL PADDING attribute,
  TABLE tags, 162
CELLSPACING attribute,
  TABLE tags, 162

client-side mapping,
  128-132
coding process for HTML,
  66-67
COLOR attribute, FONT
  tag, 101-103
color depth
   GIF files, 37
   PNG files, 38
Color Manipulation Device
  program, 190
color palettes for Web
  usage, 180
colors
   fills, 52-53
   gradients, 52-53
   RGB values, 135-137
   text, 101-103, 140-141
   tips for usage, 180
COLSPAN attribute, TD
  tags, 163
column options on Web
  pages, 160-162, 165-168
combining text styles,
  93-94
compression options for
  graphics
   JPG, 9, 22-23
   PNG, 9, 24-25
connection options for
  Web, 184
converting
   AVI movies to anima-
     tions, 158-159
   graphics for Web use,
     16-28
   image files, 30-32
Corel PhotoPaint, 191
cropping
   graphics, 34-35
   line art, 179
   photographs, 179